Lifting the Veil of Evil that Hides a Loving God

by

Branka Vukshich

TEACH Services, Inc.
P U B L I S H I N G
www.TEACHServices.com • (800) 367-1844

Copyright © 2017 Branka Vukshich

Copyright © 2022 TEACH Services, Inc.

ISBN-13: 978-1-4796-1520-9 (Paperback)

ISBN-13: 978-1-4796-1521-6 (ePub)

Library of Congress Control Number: 2022910290

TEACH Services, Inc.

P U B L I S H I N G

www.TEACHServices.com • (800) 367-1844

Table of Contents

Introduction 5

Chapter One: Anne 7

Chapter Two: Lucifer and Confusion 17

Chapter Three: The Rebellion 24

Chapter Four: People Get Involved 44

Chapter Five: More Confusion 59

Chapter Six: Jesus 71

Chapter Seven: The End of the Conflict 84

Notes 95

Table of Contents

Introduction ....

Chapter One: ... Personal Confession ....

Chapter Two: The Sabbath ....

Chapter Three: People Perish and ....

Chapter Four: ... Violent Violence ....

Chapter Five: ....

Chapter Seven: The End of the World ....

End Note ....

Introduction

You may think you hate God for a good reason. There is much suffering in the world. No one escapes. Your hatred may have brought you to the place where you cannot believe that God exists. I have attempted to read several books on *theodicy*, a fancy word for trying to understand why God allows evil. While, without exception, the reality of theodicy is part of everyone's experience, the theoretical explanations are generally outside the scope of the reading ability of the non-theologian. Frankly, some of the explanations in these philosophical, theological tomes are pretty lame.

This book is an attempt to explain in layman's language the reasons that God allows sin and suffering. I am a very simple, concrete-thinking person; if it doesn't meet the common sense test, it probably is not true. I tend to think best on paper, writing down my arguments and then critiquing them. Consequently, this layman's book, written through a Biblical lens, is in story form. Our fictional heroine, Anne, asks many of the questions that you have asked throughout your life. I sincerely hope you find the same answer that Anne did.

Chapter One

Anne

Ugh! Six o'clock and I finally reached home after a long commute. *Too late in the day*, I kept thinking. I hated the commute, but it was the price I paid for the best-paying job I could find. I needed every penny of earnings. I was ready for the weekend, happy to relax a little bit. But, in reality, I would most likely be catching up on the things left undone at home. I unlocked the door and hoped to hear some noise but instead the house was eerily quiet—again. "So, where are they?" I fumed out loud. It wasn't easy keeping track and trying to rein in three teenage boys ages 18, 16, and 13, particularly since I was raising them on my own with no help from anyone. Even when they were home, they were "semi out of control." I fed them, clothed them, and loved them intensely, but they didn't seem to respond to my care or my love. I especially worried about my middle son, Kevin, who "they" had labeled as "special needs." He spent his life trying to be like his brothers. I spent my life working, worrying, and waiting for the dreaded phone call telling me of some disaster. John, my oldest, had already been in trouble with the law—not much but enough to worry me. I knew the two oldest experimented with drugs. I was just waiting to hear that my youngest was involved too. He *was* a good student, but I didn't think that would spare him. I felt as though stuck in a great pit with no way out. Every time I tried to climb out, the sides of the pit crumbled, keeping me trapped.

The silence was broken by the ticking of the clock, an inheritance from my mom. She died young. How I hated the ticking of that clock. But, sometimes, I wanted time to speed up so that my sons' perilous teenage years would be over. The ominous ticking reminded me of the shortness of my own life. I tried not to think about the ticking— measuring my life away in noisy little segments. The house was so dreadfully quiet, the ticking ominously loud, like some scene in a horror movie where the victim is about to be ….

I shrugged. I always had stupid thoughts.

Back to reality, I tried calling Shawn, my oldest son's best friend. He was unfailingly kind to all the boys, even Kevin. Though I didn't approve of everything he did or said, unless he had a devious reason for his kindness to all the boys, I hoped they were all with Shawn. I called him. No answer. Where *were* they? They were supposed to at least text and keep me posted. I whined about it often enough, but they communicated mainly when they needed something. In our house, ignoring Mom was a teen badge of honor. We didn't even eat together much anymore. Everyone grabbed what they could when they could. But, most of the time, we at least ate breakfast together on weekends, mainly because I always cooked something special.

What should I do now to quench my continual nagging fear? Maybe there was something mindless on television I could watch to escape reality. No luck—too early. The news was still on. Slaughter was on the news. *Again*. Scenes of carnage with a bluntness designed to create outrage and cut through a viewer's sense of unreality. You could almost hear the flies buzzing over the heads of the lifeless victims piled in front of the fire-scarred humble structure. I imagined the death stench, the smell of road kill, only this time it was human, and I quickly turned off the news. *YouTube*, I thought. Up popped a report on drug abuse and the deplorable condition of American families. I could relate to that, but it wasn't exactly news to me. I scrolled through cooking and exercise programs. I lacked the energy to hunt for something more interesting—some piece of knowledge that would make my problems disappear.

Real escape was what I needed. What to do? I searched the refrigerator for some food. I wasn't really hungry. I knew that I just wanted to feel better. I slammed the door shut. *Nope. I'm not going to eat, because I'm getting fat and I don't need another problem to add to the collection. Besides, I ate a big lunch at work,* I thought to myself. I went down the escape list. I didn't have any liquor in the house because of the boys. And I had lost my taste for the nonsense of bars, so that was out. I swore off drugs before the boys were born, and I wasn't going back to that empty "problem solver." What next? Sleep? SLEEP. I was exhausted. I headed for the bedroom to try to sleep. It really *had* been a long and very humiliating day at work and an even longer workweek. Maybe I would take just *one* over-the-counter sleeping pill, just to get me over the hump. I decided not even to do that, hoping that relaxation or sleep would come quickly because I was so, so tired. Maybe at least one of the boys would be back by the time I woke up.

As I pillowed my head, the frightening TV scenes whirled through my mind. I began to rail against a God that would allow devastation, hunger, murder, disobedience to a loving parent—every form of evil—to be daily fare. God had even allowed my boys to be fatherless, but I had to admit that it was actually better to be without "good 'ole abusive Dad."

Childhood stories depicted God as love. I had read through the whole Bible at least once, but it was confusing. Anyway, I had long ago decided that those ancient myths were fantasy. High school teachers and college professors had set me straight. So had life. A loving God was a cruel joke. Philosophers and scientists proclaimed Him dead. Yet I had no one else to blame for all the trouble—mine and the world's.

> *"God, if You are there, I hate you."*

"Too bad God doesn't exist," I said out loud. "God, if You *are* there, I hate you." I was surprised by my own speech. "You don't even defend Yourself," I whimpered. Silence answered me again. "And, uh," I nearly sobbed, "If You are there, help me! I really need some help."

As I slowly relaxed, the lines memorized in childhood came to mind, "The LORD is my shepherd; I shall not want" (Ps. 23:1). Then I remembered the pile of bodies.

"Disgusting," I raged. *But maybe*, I thought, *perhaps God wasn't the monster I believed Him to be. Maybe I had missed or misunderstood something important. But it was a ridiculous thought anyway. There was no way that an all-powerful, good God could allow such a terrible state of affairs in the world. God couldn't exist. Or, if He did, maybe He was terribly evil.* I shuddered at the thought. However, being afloat in a universe ruled by mere chance was an unsatisfying alternative. It didn't make sense. What was it that funny, rather skinny pastor had said a long, long time ago? I couldn't remember exactly. Free will or something like that. But how that fit into the reality I was experiencing, I certainly couldn't tell. Eventually what I had sought for happened—a troubled sleep took over. I hated this life. Most of all, I hated God—*if* He existed.

My mind swirled from one inane theme to another. I dozed and woke up periodically, seeking again the delicious release of sleep.

The longed-for sleep was suddenly broken by a strange, blazing light that surrounded me. I was scared. I tried to look, but the intense light blinded me. What a weird dream! I willed myself to wake up, but it didn't work; the light was still there. What if this was not a dream? What if I was going crazy or dying? I started to sweat. What was the meaning of this? Despite my fear, my eyes began to adjust somewhat to the light. Weird. I smell a sweet fragrance in the

> *I was scared. I tried to look, but the intense light blinded me.*

air. Birds are singing happily. My vision improved, and I stood up. Wow! Flowers everywhere. I thought that if dead people go somewhere, this might be the place—heaven? Hell? It couldn't be hell. This place was actually very, very pleasant and peaceful. Then I panicked and said aloud, "My kids!" I began to worry about them. I had no business being in Valhalla, or wherever this was, while the boys needed me.

I was scared again. Then I realized that someone was next to me, maybe had been all along. Who was it? Maybe he or she could help me. This was stupid. I was like Dorothy in *The Wizard of Oz* trying to get home from somewhere. I could just barely see a person's outline through a bright, thick haze surrounding him or her. A melodious deep voice said, "Don't be afraid. Your children are in a safe place. They are well."

"What!" I exploded. "How do you know my children?"

"Of course I know your children," he calmly stated. Then he continued, "God respects your concerns about life—about good and evil—and He wants to answer your questions." He smiled. "Do you want answers?" He waited for me to respond.

"Sure," I said tentatively, feeling rather disoriented.

Then he said, "At the end of our journey of understanding, you will comprehend why God allows evil in the world. Your new knowledge will help you understand your own situation."

I stared at him, trying to see through the haze of obscuring light. He looked safe enough from what I could see. "Is this really happening?" I blurted out, "Or is it just a dream?"

"This is not a dream," he chuckled. "God has commissioned me to speak to you."

I paused. "You said my kids are OK?"

"The children are with Jason Dee, working on the car he just bought," said the glowing man.

Nasty kids, I thought, *showing how tough they are by not calling me—again.* I actually wanted to cry, but it didn't seem appropriate in this beautiful place.

"How do *you* know Jason?" I asked.

"I know Jason, your boys, and you. I heard you praying a short while ago. I know about your confusion," he said.

"Don't be afraid."

I froze. He heard my irreverent talk about God? "It wasn't much of a prayer. I mean, uhhh, actually I was a little angry at God. But I didn't mean it, not really. I'm sorry!" I hoped the man, who seemed more than a man, believed me.

"Don't be afraid." He smiled and paused and then slowly repeated his invitation, "Would you like the answers to your questions?"

"Of course!" I blurted out, relieved.

"Good," said my new friend. After a pause, he continued, "There *is* indeed a reason for all the misery on earth."

I started recovering my senses, trying to put the last few minutes into a logical order. *God must exist,* I thought to myself. I felt humbled, embarrassed, and still somewhat frightened, though my friend told me not to be afraid. God had been listening to all my complaints, but apparently, He didn't hate me for them. "So, I *am* in heaven?" I finally asked.

"Yes. Have your eyes adjusted completely to the light?" asked my companion.

"I can see you perfectly well now." I paused. He was a pleasure to behold. Just what I thought an angel would look like, so I asked him, "Are you an angel?"

"Yes. A son of God," he said, "And my delight is to serve Him continually."

Odd, I thought. "What's your name, anyway?" I asked.

"In your language it is 'he who is beloved of God,' but that's very long. Call me Amor-el. Since you studied French in high school, we can make it French-sounding and a lot shorter."

I thought to myself, *He knows I studied French in high school? I started to grow hot. He knows everything about me. Well, he seems to have a sense of humor. His eyes are kind and his voice gentle. I liked the twinkle in his eye. Amor-el. Amazing! It fits him.*

"I guess you know *my* name already," I said.

"Yes, Anne, I do," he said slowly and then paused, "Are you feeling more settled?"

"I guess so," I answered.

"Good. Let's start by going for a walk." We headed down a path and walked for a few minutes. It was so overwhelmingly lovely. Birds. Mild floral perfume. Sunshine. A perfect temperature. Then in the distance were a group of beautiful beings looking very intently at one in the group who was talking. I had never seen such strikingly handsome beings before. All were youthful. I couldn't call them people. They were too perfect, and they seemed to glow. We walked by the most beautiful houses made of vines and other growing plants. There were flowers intertwined in the walls and everywhere the air carried different varieties of floral perfume. The beautiful beings greeted us as we walked along. They seemed to know who I was, and I sensed that they genuinely liked me. There were animals and birds of every description. A man was playing with a giant cat of some kind. Others were resting and talking, sitting close to grazing animals. Still others were involved in what appeared to be some kind of projects.

> *Maybe it was all an evil trick. But I had no other option than to go forward on this journey.*

I stared at Amor-el again and thought, *Well, if God's servant is so appealing, maybe I didn't need to be afraid of God either.* Or maybe it was all an evil trick. But I had no other option than to go forward on this journey with my companion because I wanted to find out what he knew.

"Are you at peace, Anne?"

"Yes," I said. "No one seems to be afraid. No one is hurried or angry. Even the animals and birds are friendly. This is absolutely awesome. There seems to be peace everywhere. Somehow I sense that everyone and everything loves. I'm astounded." I paused. "Yes, I'm at peace, but it seems too perfect to be true." Then I asked, "Why does everyone seem to glow?"

"It is the visible presence of God's Spirit," answered Amor-el.

"Oh," I said and thought, *Something else that is very different about this place—glowing people, I mean beings.*

"You have grasped what you've seen so far splendidly well. Now I'm going to take you back in time and show you the only thing that mars the happiness of our existence— the very beginning of our problem. Without this revelation, you cannot understand what is happening on earth."

Our problem. Huh, I thought. *He doesn't live in our earthly hell. Why would it be our problem?*

"Wait," I said. "This just doesn't seem fair. You've brought me to this place that is absolutely, I mean absolutely, glorious. If it wasn't for my kids, I would just stay here forever. But many of the smartest people on earth don't even believe that such a place exists or that God exists. How can God just go on not telling anyone the truth? It really doesn't seem fair."

"I understand," Amor-el said. "You will comprehend shortly. But actually, God *has* given you ample evidence of His existence. He made your intricately balanced world. Have you ever known *anything* to come of itself without a creator?"

"I guess automatic, self-creation doesn't make sense. God *must* exist," I said. I had always leaned toward belief in a Creator which caused me great deal of confusion because of all the evil in the world. "So the real issue is not whether God exists, but what He is like."

"Indeed. That was our dilemma too," smiled Amor-el.

Indeed, I thought to myself.

"For this reason, God has revealed Himself to men in a remarkable way," Amor-el said.

"He has not!" I shot back. *Oops*, I thought. I caught myself. *I used to not believe in heaven, either. Maybe I should back off a little bit.* Sheepishly, I said, "You mean the Bible? I used to think the Bible was true, but there are so many contradictions and things that just don't make sense, that I just can't believe it." I stopped, deferring to Amor-el's greater knowledge, "*Should* I believe the Bible?"

"You'll have time to make up your mind as we journey on. No one can or should force you to believe. You must believe or not believe based on the weight of evidence," said Amor-el. "God never forces anyone against his will to believe."

I thought, *I'm going to be deeply humiliated on this trip. But better to be humiliated than dead wrong. The truth is that I actually want to be wrong in my understanding of God.* Hope sprang up in my heart.

"I'm ready to go on," I said, "though I don't like the thought of a problem in this beautiful place. I'm ready to try to understand."

CHAPTER TWO

Lucifer and Confusion

Our journey began to the left of us. Amor-el encouraged me to ask any questions that I wanted to ask.

"Anne, look over there and you will find the beginning of the answer to all your questions. You will see Michael the Prince, and Lucifer."

"Whoa. Really? As a kid, my Sunday school teacher told us that Lucifer is an evil angel. He doesn't *look* evil. He is exceedingly handsome." I paused to scan my brain. "So, I think I know who Lucifer is, but who is Michael?"[1] I said.

"Our Prince Michael was one with God the Father from eternity," said Amor-el. "He is without beginning and without end. He created everything that was ever created."

"How do you know?" I interrupted and smiled. "Were you there?" *Gotcha*, I thought.

"Because He said so," Amor-el chuckled. "Obviously, no angel observed the very first creation. But we've seen many other creations since then. Earthlings are understandably an unbelieving, skeptical people. But the angels have *no* reason to doubt Prince Michael's word but every reason to believe His *every* word. In your world, people are convicted of crimes in court based on evidence and not always solid facts. Isn't that so? Conviction is often based on the credibility of a witness. Michael is a very credible witness."

Got me, I thought. I took a good look at Lucifer, then at Michael, and then at Lucifer again.

"And Lucifer[2] is the same Lucifer that I read about in the Bible as a kid, right?" I asked.

"Indeed. His name signifies that he bears 'light' or the knowledge of God to others. He is a created being—one that bore a great deal of responsibility in God's kingdom," explained Amor-el.

"Amor-el means 'beloved of God.' Lucifer means 'light bearer.' What does Michael mean?" I asked.

"Michael means, 'who is like God?'" said Amor-el. "The Prince actually has many names because one name cannot encompass His grandeur. The Prince refers to Himself as 'the Son of God,' signifying His intimate relationship to God."

"But how can Prince Michael be the 'Son' of God if He *is* God? Is He a son or God?"

Amor-el replied with reverence, "Though He is God, 'Son' refers to the form that He has taken for the benefit of created beings. Love does whatever is best for the person one loves. Because God is overwhelmingly magnificent and grand, Michael told us that They, the Holy Ones, saw that creatures needed a Being who resembles them. One who is not surrounded by the overwhelming power that emanates from our Father's very being. *We,* the created, need a Being to communicate God's love in ways that we can understand. The Son resembled the other 'sons' of God." Amor-el paused. "In humility, He became like us. Then, to aid us further, God put His other representative, the Holy Spirit, within His creatures. He is God's instant communication to all."

Oh, I thought, *the angels' shining light.* Then I said, "You know, that's really a kind, loving thing to do." It made sense, and I hoped it was true. So, I had to ask Amor-el, "But wouldn't it be better if the Father also became more like His created beings so that you could relate easily to the Father as well as the Son?"

"You might think so. But in the presence of the Father is a place where infinite love is 'felt' yet combined with magnificent 'power.' When I am in His presence, I have the sense of security knowing that both power and love are in our Father. Anne, God makes no mistakes. In His loving providence, God knows that we need to understand both the power of our Father and the humility of God manifested in the Son who humbles Himself to call us brothers. Human scholars give the Holy Ones the name 'Trinity.'"

"Trinity[3] is an idea that we on earth struggle with," I said. I thought for a moment and realized that I might have to change my mind about the character of God. "Huh. The Trinity really *demonstrates* the love and character of God who is so humble that He conforms Himself to meet the needs of His creation."

"You are beginning to learn," smiled Amor-el.

"Tell me more about the Holy Spirit,"[4] I requested.

"The blessed Holy Spirit is what ties each of His creatures directly to God. We didn't even understand fully the blessedness of the Holy Spirit until the great rebellion began. But we will talk more about that later," said Amor-el.

During our conversation, I was also watching the two bright figures, Lucifer and Michael, as they spoke to each other. My eyes had to adjust again to see them distinctly, but I clearly heard their voices. I searched my mind, trying to remember everything I had heard on earth about the Son of God and Lucifer. It was incredible that they *really* existed. I tried to make a quick reassessment of all my past assumptions, but there wasn't time. I concentrated on the voices so I wouldn't miss anything.

"Our Father and I have laid plans for a new world,"[5] said Michael. "It will be a new type of creation, a totally new order of beings. As usual, the angelic host will take part in this creation. Our new brothers will have all the capabilities of the other worlds but with some differences."

"Differences?" said Lucifer. "My Lord Michael, the angelic host will be delighted! But what kind of differences?"

Prince Michael responded, "We shall make them male and female. Together they will have the ability to reproduce. A child will form in the body of the female. Both parents will care for and nurture the child as it grows. Thus they will form units called families, with a mother and father—parents—caring for their offspring. The parents will raise their little ones who will be born with an inheritance from both parents and with very little innate knowledge. The parents will teach them lessons of love and devotion, tying their young closely to God and to each other."

A beautiful smile came over Lucifer's face. "How interesting. How lovely. *And* how absolutely novel."

Prince Michael continued, "We will call them humans. Not only will the humans be able to reproduce but so will other forms of life in this world we are creating. The world is designed as a continual learning experience for our new brothers. Their intellect will develop day by day; consequently, they will grow continually—eternally. As they form families and bear children, they will learn to appreciate God more and more, understanding by their own experience the Creator's love for His creation. Our human relatives will be sustained by eating the fruit of trees. Eating will remind them of their dependence on God. Humans will eat from one type of tree; animals will eat other forms of vegetation. For labor and study, they will work, tending a garden for six days and then, in harmony with the universal law, they will rest on the seventh day—

enjoying special time for contemplation and communion with God and each other. These are all vital to help them grow toward a deeper understanding of the Eternal."

When their conversation ended, I saw Lucifer bow low and then rise up and embrace Michael. But it was more than an embrace. It was an intense exchange of affirmation and love between the two. Lucifer left and went to speak to a group of angels. Michael entered into a magnificent building where Amor-el told me the Father was physically present. A magnificent light shone out from the building. I had never seen, nor could I have imagined, a space such as this. There were no exterior walls, only pillars supporting the structure above. It was an expansive building, but from what I could see, it looked intimate. Peace and love seemed to hover in the vicinity. I saw a great number of angels there, going in and out—all engaged in some activity.

"Can we go in there?" I asked.

"You cannot enter in your present condition," Amor-el shook his head. "The presence of God would overwhelm your human nature. You could not survive. But, perhaps, someday you will be able to enter."

I was stunned. "Then why did you bring me here? What is Prince Michael doing in there?" I asked.

"Michael and His Father are in communication. No one must hear the words they speak to one another," said Amor-el. "They tell us that there are some things that even angels cannot yet fully understand."

I frowned at the thought of secrecy. "Only the two of them talking together? Don't you ever wonder what They say?" I asked with a semi-sneer that I tried to hide from Amor-el, but the sneer escaped in my voice.

Amor-el smiled, "No. Angels are grateful for the privilege of life, for daily joys and work to do for others. We trust God because we are convinced that They *always* act in our best interests. Our Father, Prince Michael, and the Holy Spirit would never lie to us or harm us in any way. No, we do not wonder what they are talking about." He paused, "Not anymore. But as you know by now, there was a time when even inhabitants of heaven were confused about the true meaning of 'love' and about God's character. Lucifer began to express open doubts about the character of the Holy Ones. You need to realize that while God loves us supremely, because His love, foreknowledge and understanding is perfect, we obey His every will. Not by compulsion but out of love and gratitude. Still, we were confused by Satan's accusations."

"Wow! Confusion. The same as humans!" I was exuberant. I was slowly losing my skepticism and had trouble maintaining my usual disbelief in the light of Amor-el's ardor and transparency.

"Well, never *exactly* the same as humans," said Amor-el. Loyal angels have never transgressed God's law, never personally experienced lawlessness or the need for mercy. But humans have the actual *experience* in your very being."

"I don't get it," I said.

"You will as we go on," answered Amor-el.

I paused and returned to the issue of confusion. "So, *you* doubted God's character and what Prince Michael was saying to you about Himself?" I asked.

"Yes. I doubted but remained loyal," said Amor-el, "I, and all the loyal angels, wondered if there was some truth to what Lucifer was saying about God. But only after we observed the events at the murder of Prince Michael on earth did we completely understand the answers to our questions."

"Murder of Prince Michael? On earth? Am I supposed to know something about this?" I asked.

"You know Him as Jesus," he said.

"Oh," I said. "Of course." Then I paused. "Well, I can see why the understanding of angels and humans could never be 'exactly' the same. You beings in heaven—angels—I guess you are *all* angels, aren't you? I'm sorry. I'm still trying to piece all this together," I breathed out. "Anyway, you understand the earth's entire history while we humans are very confused about some basic issues. You obviously see things differently than we do. And then the peace and security that you experience in heaven is *so* different from the way we live on earth."

"Peace and security," sighed Amor-el. "Loyal heavenly beings have come to delight in peace and security. Something we didn't even know that we had until the turmoil—the rebellion."

"*Had*?" I asked, still very confused.

"Yes, heaven is peaceful now, but heaven has known turmoil and anguish. It is actually the place where the horror you experience on earth began."

"Oh, come on now! How could this peaceful, beautiful place be the beginning of our horror on earth?" I asked. "I haven't seen anything remotely approaching horrible!"

"Let's look back into history again," said Amor-el.

CHAPTER THREE

The Rebellion

"This is how it started—the horror. You will have to observe and listen carefully," instructed Amor-el gently.

"But I haven't seen anything here remotely like horror," I whispered to Amor-el.

"No need to whisper. Ask anything you like, boldly," he replied. "What you see and hear will be confusing initially because circumstances don't appear as they are. Lucifer will make accusations that seem logical. Listen."

> *"This is how it started—the horror. You will have to observe and listen carefully."*

I looked and saw Lucifer and about forty angels gathered together. They all looked toward Lucifer with deference.

Lucifer beamed a glorious smile. He was strikingly good-looking, and I continued to feel drawn to him. It was hard not to feel positive toward someone so physically appealing. I kept trying to remind myself to be suspicious, realizing who he really was. He spoke, "Recently, our Prince Michael revealed to me the plans for a new creation on a planet called earth. At first, I accepted the event with joy, *but* I have been analyzing the basic attributes of this new race of people, and I have some important questions to ask you. I want to get *your* opinion on my thoughts."

"Of course, as always, we want to hear what you have to say," said one of the angels.

"Let's walk over to the river and sit under the trees. Then we'll talk," said Lucifer. "What I'm going to say is very serious, and it may be a little unsettling but unusually insightful. Lovingly, I tell you that I only have everyone's benefit in mind. You are the exalted leaders of the vast heavenly host and I wanted to start with you so that you can convey to your subleaders and so on."

Shortly, they reached the river.

"What is it? It must be very important," said one of the angels. "Your face reveals intense thinking *as usual*," smiled the angel. "There must be a challenging project ahead or something of that nature. What is it?"

Lucifer smiled a winsome smile. He said solemnly, looking intently at the other angels, "Have you ever considered that God should give His creatures *total* freedom? Not only should angels have total freedom, I feel that this new race should have total freedom and liberty."

"Total freedom?" asked an angel who looked stunned. There was a noticeable stirring of the group. "Whatever do you mean? We are free. We *are* at total liberty. The humans, too, will be at total liberty. Lucifer, what do you mean?"

"Freedom, ah, liberty," intoned Lucifer shaking his handsome head majestically. "What beautiful words. This freedom, this liberty is what I wanted to talk to you about. Consider this. When God creates, He implants in every creature His Spirit. He puts into them His very thoughts by this means. You know how we all live. You understand the intimate connection between each being and God. We constantly express our gratitude to God by serving Him and His creation, putting others above ourselves; God's ubiquitous Spirit rules every aspect of our very lives."

There was a stir among the angels as many looked questioningly at their neighbors.

Lucifer held up his hand. "I understand," he said, "but I must express this thought for the good of *all* creation, for the very stability of heaven and even for the good of God. If His creatures are unhappy, dissatisfied in some way, it will only create instability in heaven. I believe God should listen very closely to us."

There was silence—a painful silence. I began to understand what Amor-el had cautioned me about. It seemed that Lucifer was pitting himself against God but in a very artful way. I listened intently.

Amor-el explained, "Lucifer used the name God meaning the Father, Prince Michael, and the Holy Spirit. But angels understood that the Son was the near representative of God to us and the One to be communicated with."

Lucifer then continued, "Let's be reasonable. We act the way we do because we have *no* other choice. We are created to do exactly as God directs us." He stopped again, letting his words sink in. This time, there was a shocked look on the face of *every* angel.

"I understand your emotion," said Lucifer, raising his hands. "I also felt this way when I first realized God's design might not be perfect, might not lend itself to total liberty," Lucifer said and then continued, "But at some point we must understand that a creature becomes *so* elevated, *so* refined, *so* educated into the goodness and greatness of God that that very goodness lies *within us*. At such a point of elevation, do we really need God to direct us continually?"

A pained, stunned look appeared on some of the angels' faces but others just listened with no visible emotion. Finally, one said, "But I *want* to carry out the desires of God. I want to do *all* His will."

"God's wishes are always good and perfect," another angel said with emotion. "I just don't understand, Lucifer."

"Of course," said Lucifer, "We *want* to do these good things. And why? Because we, ourselves, by ourselves, in and of ourselves, are perfect and good. We need no further direction from anyone outside of ourselves. Suppose, for some reason, someone decided it would be best *not* to follow God's Spirit."

"Now, Lucifer, how can that be?" asked an angel with a puzzled look on his face.

"Listen and I will tell you," Lucifer countered. "Listen. Why *must* we always give to others? Does God Himself do that?"

"Of course He does," several angels spoke out.

Lucifer smiled. "Just think about it. We serve Him constantly. We do whatever *He* wishes," said Lucifer.

"Why shouldn't we? We want to do His wishes. Besides, what would we want to do other than give?" said a dark-haired angel. "Giving makes me happy. What other choice do we have? *Not* to give and do for each other?"

"Oh, giving is marvelous—the way it should be! But you raise the all-important issue. The issue of choice," said Lucifer. "Of course. That is exactly the question! What other choice is there?" said Lucifer.

"Whatever are you talking about Lucifer?" an angel asked.

Lucifer paused for a moment. "*Here* is the choice we can have. I envision a universe where it is *first* to ourselves and then to others. From our abundance we give—and we give abundantly, overflowing, even more graciously than the way that God instructs us to give. We do it because it is right and good, a decision we make on our own. If we put ourselves first, as God Himself does, our growth would be significantly improved—expanded, like God Himself. If God continually directs us, what choice is there? None. Are we not sufficiently able to make choices about what is proper? About what is beneficial?"

"This is quite a unique approach," said an angel. "Your analysis is actually foundational. I never thought about it. You have opened my understanding about this primary issue. Go on, Lucifer. I feel that such a shift would not ever be against God's will, but it would elevate *us* to an even higher level. We would be even closer to God—a parallel experience with that of God."

"I don't see how it can be. You say a choice could be counter to God's will?" said another.

"It is a possibility," said Lucifer. "Certainly remote, but what of it? Angels know right from wrong by their very nature, by their training, and by communication with one another. We would never hurt one another. However, God is so lofty and exalted, can He understand us or our needs and desires? Decisions should come from angels and not God."

"I must interrupt! How can you question God?" asked another. "He has given us everything. Life itself! What are you saying? Of course we live by God's Spirit. It is my desire to be one with Him continually. God cannot be 'not right.'"

"Not right?" I asked.

"We did not then have a word for 'wrong,'" said Amor-el. "Very astute of you to pick that up."

My gaze shifted back to Lucifer.

"Hear me, my dear brothers," said Lucifer, sounding a little bit frustrated. "I have thought hard and long about this. I don't propose to change any major way of living. We *need* to love one another. We *need* to serve each other. We *need* to give to each other. But what is wrong in loving ourselves first, just as God loves Himself first?"

"God loves Himself first? That would make Him a teller of—what would you call it? A teller of 'not truth'—because *He* has put it into our minds to love others first, not ourselves first. That love to others *must* be from Him."

"Of course," said Lucifer. "It fits into His plan nicely. When we put others first, we, of necessity, put Him first. It suits Him quite well. Everything is done for *Him*. Everyone obeys Him without even considering that in everything that we do, we are putting God first and putting ourselves under his control. Michael gives us instructions. And we obey."

"Lucifer, I love you as a brother," said another angel, "but you are not thinking clearly. God does not teach us to do one thing and then does another Himself. That would not be just. We obey Him because He knows what is best for us and because He always does what is just and true and right."

Lucifer's handsome face grew pensive. "How can God know what is best for *us*? We are angels and He is God. Can He feel what we feel? Does He understand our situation?" asked Lucifer.

Another angel retorted, "Of course He understands our feelings. He understands *everything*. Prince Michael is our Lord, but He is also our brother. He is God. And He loves *us* entirely. Totally. So we love Him the same way. Think of all He has given us! We should obey Him if only out of gratitude, seeing that everything we have comes from Him."

"Everything? That's exactly what I mean. Yes, everything we have comes from God, but He *hasn't* given us everything," said Lucifer.

There was yet another stir among the angels. They looked puzzled and some looked distressed.

"Listen to me, dear brothers, while I explain. If God, the Son, took on the form such as we have, and that He has now, in order to communicate more effectively with us—or so the Son has told us—then why can't God give an angel power akin to that of God? He creates through us, but why doesn't He share *with* us more of his godly powers? Why am I, Lucifer, excluded from the conversations between the Father and Michael? Angels are quite capable of accepting this responsibility. Especially those that have dwelt in close communion with God for eons and eons." There was silence among the group. Lucifer continued with a beautiful, handsome smile on his face, "Isn't God selfishly withholding what He could easily give? Isn't He putting Himself first?"

"Hmmm," murmured one angel, "I am beginning to see your point."

"I also understand your thinking, Lucifer." The angel speaking paused, "But I cannot agree. God has bestowed great honor upon you. You have the privilege of being often in His presence. Why aren't you content with what you have? Why have you left His presence, your post of duty, to come and speak to us against God?"

Another angel objected. "Are you asking for power equal to God? God's ultimate power is not yours to have! No one can or should ever be equal to God. There is *no* reason for it. We are all honored by God. We have the privilege of being in His presence. We are all content. We have the privilege of serving God and others. Are we unhappy? No. Do we lack anything? No. I see your reasoning as somehow, somehow ... I don't even have the word for it—not giving God honor. It could lead to events that would change our happy condition. We have never had anything but total agreement in heaven."

Lucifer's face brightened, "Brilliantly said! No one has ever disagreed with God. How do you know I *shouldn't* disagree with God? That *we* shouldn't disagree with God? And how do you know I can't reach a level closer to God?

God can do anything. He can bestow this honor on me. And on you too! If only God weren't thinking just of Himself."

Again, there was a stunned silence. Lucifer stood up once more, raising his hands to quiet the group.

"Oh, listen," said Lucifer, "I'm not talking about somehow replacing God or giving Him less honor, but I *am* talking about getting the honor due to the superb angelic host." Lucifer motioned to those around him, "Nothing would change except that we would *all* be more glorious—more exalted. This is not just for me. God would ultimately share His position *and* His power with all of us, but He could retain His exalted position."

"For what purpose would God do that? For what reason would God make such a change? Would you be closer to God than Prince Michael Himself?" asked an angel.

"The Father says that Michael is also God. Listen again as I repeat myself," Lucifer said. "If God became the Prince in form like us, then why can't an angel become like God? Either Michael is not *really* God or God does not want to share His position with us because He wants it only for Himself—and Michael. He wants to order everything to His liking. Just exactly what He is telling *us* not to do."

"Look at this new creation on earth," continued Lucifer. "They will be encumbered with God's Holy Spirit, mindlessly following God's every whim, just as all the rest of creation does. They will not be allowed to think apart from God's will. I desire freedom for them."

The dark-haired angel spoke up again, "If anyone other than Lucifer were saying these things I would question it. Lucifer, you have had the privilege of knowing God intimately. You are the one who stands with Prince Michael in the presence of God." He paused, "Can it be?

Is God really requiring of us something that He Himself does not perform?"

There was silence. Finally, an angel spoke up solemnly, "We must speak to Prince Michael Himself about these things. God's Spirit within me objects to such thoughts—I feel in such a way as I have never felt before."

Lucifer smiled. "Agreed, and the feeling is not unpleasant. It is the feeling of freedom." Lucifer's face seemed to lighten. "Think for yourself without depending on God. He knows what we are talking about already," said Lucifer. "God knows everything. He has not interrupted us; everything continues as it always has—the mountains are still standing, the heavenly bodes are still in their orbits. We are still alive—everything is intact—so He must *know* that I am correct. It is just a matter of time until He accedes to my—no, *our*—wishes. If *all* the angels agree, He will give us what we want—quickly. Perhaps immediately. Please understand, I am not asking for God's place. That is His and His alone. But I want to be acknowledged by God for the powers of insight and goodness that I have *and* the ones that I have developed through my own diligence and work—are not my own achievements, created by *my* efforts, equal to what God initially gave me? With one hand God gives, but then He puts a limit on what we can accomplish. That is not right, good, or equal."

"No. The Holy Spirit within me does not agree with you. I will not join with you," said an angel.

Another said, "I must speak personally to Prince Michael about this. I have never experienced this emotion before, but it feels very, very—it feels very, uh, uh—I don't have a word for it. Not right, yes, not right."

"I have the same feeling," said another.

An angel standing in the back of the group spoke out, "Well, I have the 'feeling,' but I think Lucifer is right!"

Lucifer beamed, "I *am* right. Stay with me. Don't let your uneducated *feelings* hinder you—these very feelings are instilled by God. You'll soon get over your incorrect feelings, and certainly don't allow yourself to be overpowered by God's Spirit. Use your *own* intellect. It will not and *cannot* lead you incorrectly. For the rest of you, go ahead and speak to Michael about my just concerns. But remember if you agree with Michael, remember also that His advice is tainted, that He has the desire to keep power over you. We must speak to Him instead about our impending improvement. Brothers, we must put together a plan. Let us speak frequently to each other. We must be united in our efforts. Michael will surely see to it that we meet with Him shortly."

"Lucifer, I had a thought. God could just replace us if we rise up against His will," said an angel.

"God would never do such a thing. He loves us," said another.

Lucifer smiled. "You are beginning to understand. Does He love us? Or does He only love us only while we obey Him?" said Lucifer. "Michael has already warned me that if I continue in this path, it will lead to my annihilation, my extinction."

There was an uproar. The angels all cried one thing or another. I couldn't understand what they were saying. For the first time in my short visit, I experienced unrest and unhappiness in heaven. I was taken aback.

Lucifer waved them to silence and then spoke, "But I have thought this through. I am even willing to risk my own death for the freedom of all of you," said Lucifer. "What good is this life to me, or to any of us, without absolute freedom?"

There was a murmur among the angels.

Lucifer held up his hand. "But that will not be," said Lucifer. "We need only be united. God will give us what is right. I have *that* much faith in Him. God is not totally without honor."

There was a shocked look on the face of the angels. One shouted out, "Without honor! How can you say that about our loving God?"

"Lucifer, if God said that your line of thinking will lead to your extinction, why don't you believe Him and stop? Do you think that God should allow you to live forever in opposition to Him?" said another angel.

Lucifer smiled, "Well said. Do you see that He is unfair? If anyone opposes Him, there is a threat of extinction. I believe He is trying to make me do what my mind tells me is not right. He is exercising force against me," said Lucifer.

"Force? What do you mean? You mean the power that we exert to move rock and heavy objects?" said an angel.

"Force in this sense is compelling someone under pain of punishment to do what he would not normally do," said Lucifer. "I would normally follow my conclusions and act accordingly, but I cannot except I put my very life at risk."

"God would not do such a thing. Do you believe that God is telling you something that is not true?" asked another angel.

I couldn't help asking Amor-el what was on my mind, "You know, what Lucifer is saying makes sense. Is God really selfish? Does He really force angels into doing His will on pain of extinction?"

"We weren't sure," said Amor-el. "Lucifer presented a reasonable argument. Prince Michael met with us often and there were many, many discussions similar to what you have just heard. Lucifer and his followers contended that angels naturally do what is right because they were naturally endowed by God with the ability to understand and because of their superior intellectual abilities they could, through reason alone, decide what is just and good.

Lucifer and his angels argued that they didn't need the guidance of the Holy Spirit and felt that the Holy Spirit kept them in bondage to a lower level of existence that God had unfairly consigned them to. They further said that if angels discussed and agreed to something, *whatever* they decided would be good. God's answer was that *only* He understood good and evil, and God told us that the end of the path that Lucifer was taking leads to unhappiness and finally to destruction. Evil, acting against God's will, was a totally new concept to us."

"Help me understand this," I said. "Evil is anything against God's will. I always conceived of evil as theft, murder, lying—you know—really bad stuff."

"It is bad stuff," said Amor-el. "But worse still is acting against God's will. God is perfect love so anything that is not His will is evil. I know this is a new idea to you, and we will talk about it more later."

"Good. I need time to think about the definition of evil," I said.

"So did the heavenly host. This experience with evil was new to us. We had to invent the words 'rebellion,' 'disobedience,' and many others. We began to understand, as we had not before, that God had a law, a principle by which we lived and that Lucifer was introducing an opposite principle, but, perhaps, a viable one. God's principle is self-sacrificing love and Lucifer's is self-centeredness. These are the only two possible principles in the universe and they are mutually exclusive—we came to learn that soon enough."

"So, I have another question," I said. "At first, was God just trying to frighten Lucifer into obedience? Right? It must have been a truly awful experience for you angels to believe that Lucifer would actually, really die."

"God does not use force in any way," Amor-el said. "The use of force is contrary to all of God's principles, but

He persuades by speaking truth. This truth was frightening to the loyal angels. It was shocking to us that God would allow death to come to any of His beings if His law of self-sacrificing love was not adhered to. We truly did not understand how death, in any way, was in keeping with the character of God." Amor-el continued, "These new ideas of Lucifer's were totally shocking to us. All heaven was in turmoil. God pled with Lucifer to give up his rebellion. The Lord explained that, for the good of the universe, He could never change His foundational order, His law. He explained that if angels accepted the principle that they could determine what was right and wrong without the guidance of the Holy Spirit, they abandoned His principle of self-sacrificing love. Self-sacrificing love—a manifestation of God's very nature, is shared by His creation through the indwelling of the Holy Spirit but that we couldn't even fully understand the depth of the principle. God told us that creatures didn't have the ability to understand all things as God did and that the laws and strictures that creatures imposed on themselves was not a substitute for the indwelling of the Holy Spirit which tied all of God's creation together in a harmonious bond of love. God, furthermore, warned Satan that great evil would result from his determination to rebel against divine authority."

> *"Tears are not shameful," said Amor-el. "Not to feel pity and love is shameful."*

Toward the end of his explanation, Amor-el's voice sounded funny. I looked up at him and saw tears in his eyes. "I didn't know that angels could cry," I stammered. "Oh! I didn't mean to be rude and say that! It just slipped out."

"Tears are not shameful," said Amor-el. "*Not* to feel pity and love is shameful. Angels laugh and now we have learned to cry. We have emotions, deep emotions, just like humans, only more so because we have the Holy Spirit living within us in His fullness. We have no need to hide our emotions as humans do." He paused. "It makes me emotional even now to speak of the rebellion. Anne, to the same measure that we love, we feel the pain. I know it is hard for you to understand, but angels are in more emotional agony than humans even though humans suffer physical pain and emotional abuse and we do not. We have lost one-third of our brothers because they followed Lucifer," Amor-el's voice quavered. "And we see people being rebellious on earth, causing sorrow to God and the heavenly beings."

I couldn't believe that I was starting to feel sorry for Amor-el. He lived in security and I did not, but I began to comprehend his hurt and agony over this huge problem of evil. I was beginning to see how foundational a problem sin is.

Amor-el started speaking again, "Those of us who continued to be loyal to God were still confused. We loved our angel brethren. But we accepted wholeheartedly their banishment from heaven after the murder of our Prince Michael. Until the murder, there was a haze over our understanding. Until the murder, we wondered if Lucifer might be right, though we continued to live in harmony with God. What God said to us sounded correct, but Lucifer's accusations made God seem like what you earthlings call a 'tyrant.' Many of us determined to trust God based on our previous experiences with Him. We did not rebel, but we were confused. Very confused."

"You know," I mused, "I'm thinking about Lucifer and his demands. My children do that to me all the time. They ask for something absurd and then blame me for not giving them what they reasonably know they shouldn't have. They try to make me feel guilty."

"Yes, we wondered if the trouble was because God would not give Lucifer what he wanted or if the problem was with Lucifer," said Amor-el.

There was a comfortable silence as each of us pondered our own thoughts. I broke the silence with a burning question.

"Well, why didn't God just kill Lucifer?" I asked. Then I realized the implications for the surviving angels who would remember Lucifer, so I added: "God could have killed you all and started over again and programmed the new creation without the ability to rebel." I felt somewhat ashamed of the thought; justifying it, I said, "Think of all the suffering Lucifer has caused. He even contaminated the loyal angels. If I were in charge, *I* would have killed him a long time ago. I'd like to torch him right now if he really is the cause of all the problems and suffering on earth."

Amor-el began to answer, but I motioned to let him know I had a more urgent question. He *had* said that I could ask anything I wanted to. "Now something doesn't quite make sense here. Why would a perfect, all-knowing God even create someone who would end up rebelling against Him? I heard Lucifer's arguments, but after experiencing this place for a while, I knew he wasn't lacking anything. Why would he rebel? I don't get it, though I am ashamed to admit that his arguments kind of resonated with me."

"That is a puzzling question, isn't it?" Amor-el responded. "Rebellion against God is truly a mystery. If there were an explanation—some overriding reason for it—there might be an excuse. And yet it happened. In answer to your first question, God ordained that creatures have the ability to make choices because it is the nature of His love. Without choice, there can be no true love. But tell me, why are *your* children rebelling against you?" He paused for a moment and then added softly. "And why did you rebel against your parents?"

I blushed as I considered my past. "I've … I guess I've given that a lot of thought lately because the boys remind me of myself as a teenager. Something you seem to know all about already." I smiled. Remembering the implications of my companion knowing all about my entire history, the smile left my face, but I continued, "Well, I think it's just autonomy—the desire to be one's own boss *and* looking for perfect love. I think it is a fear of being denied some experience or pleasure that others are having or appear to be having. I think, in large part, it is because we feel that we can discern what it good or bad for ourselves and that we can easily change course if the consequences become too difficult. I know my parents suffered a lot because of me, and I understand them better now that I'm dealing with my own children. I actually wouldn't have a problem with the boys taking greater charge of their lives *if* they were mature enough to make wise decisions and handle their own affairs. But they're not. So, we get into a lot of disagreements."

"A very similar situation," said Amor-el. "Autonomy, growing out of Lucifer's self-centeredness is his goal, *and* as we later understood—but did not know to start with—a deep jealousy of the Prince. The loyal angels have a difficult time understanding this overriding desire for autonomy and hatred for the Prince. God met Lucifer's every need—a perfect environment, the ability to plan creatively and carry out his plans, companionship—everything. He was closer to God than any created being. But as horrible as this experience with sin has been, we thank God for making us in such a way that we *can* rebel. Even though it has been tremendously painful for God, the principle of choice is so important to God that He made us with that ability. Without choice, there can be no true love and devotion. In this, God has given us a most glorious gift. God created men and angels in His own image—with the power of choice."

"Before I answer your other question...." said Amor-el.

"Which was? I can't remember anymore," I said.

"Why did God create Lucifer and the rebellious angels knowing they would cause disaster?" said Amor-el.

"Oh. Yeah," I said.

"First, answer *my* question," said Amor-el. "I know that you understood before deciding to have children that they create problems. Why did you then decide to give birth to children?"

I paused and did some thinking. "I was looking forward to loving my children and having them love me. I wanted a special relationship with them. I trusted that they would respond to my love." I stopped talking for a few moments. "OK, I get it. God is love and He loves those He created but He loved enough to give us all free will—even Lucifer. I really do understand. It just took me a while to think it through." I paused. "But why didn't God erase Lucifer *after* He saw that he was a rebel and would just cause a lot of problems?"

"Ah!" breathed Amor-el with a smile. "Had God eliminated Lucifer, the loyal angels *would* have believed that Lucifer was telling the truth about God. We would have thought that God just whimsically kills those that question Him, proving that God is selfish, just as Lucifer had pictured Him to us. We would have continued to serve God but only from fear—a manner of life that is totally unacceptable to God and to us. No, God has a much better way—a very painful but perfect way. He is allowing rebellion to extinguish itself. You will understand the extinguishment more fully as we continue."

"To extinguish itself?" I thought for a moment, then said, "Oh, on earth! I think it is beginning to make more sense. Let me see if I can verbalize it all. When our first parents sided with Lucifer by disobeying Him, they accepted self-centeredness as their inner law, the principal they then lived by. They rejected God's Spirit, just as Lucifer had, and were left to themselves—without the Holy Spirit—to choose right from wrong based on their own reasoning. They were in the same spiritual mode as Lucifer. Isn't that what Lucifer promised? '[Y]e shall be as gods, knowing good and evil' (Gen. 3:5)—autonomy, self-centeredness instead of being God-centered. I get it!"

We were silent for a moment; I finally had to continue. "I'm getting it intellectually, but now I feel like cosmic roadkill—a helpless victim of some huge spiritual battle that I had no part in beginning. It doesn't seem fair. Don't you realize how much the people on earth have suffered because of this? Haven't you seen the carnage, the fear, the horror? Does God hate us so much because our first parents were rebellious that He allowed us to be used as pawns in this cosmic argument?"

Amor-el winced and then said, "God does not hate you. God is love. Had God a selfish nature as Lucifer imputed to Him, He would be as you just said, but God is unselfish, lavish love."

Amor-el continued, "I think I understand how you feel about being in the middle of this controversy. But if God hadn't allowed rebellion to continue, you would not be alive." Amor-el intently looked at me and implored, "Anne, rise above your selfish nature. I, for one, would be grateful for the privilege to be loyal to God in the enemy's territory and exonerate His holy name. There was no other way to create the permanent and necessary loyalty to God other than allowing the freedom of choice and a full revelation of God's character through an understanding of the pain that rebellion creates and to let sin run its course. Remember, God did not leave you alone in this controversy. He is not sitting in a detached way while you suffer. He joins in with you every day. All heaven is involved in this controversy, and He gave you the greatest gift possible. He sent Prince Michael. He is called Emmanuel in the Bible—God with humanity (Matt. 1:23). Since the inception of sin, God has suffered tremendously. God lost many beloved children. He loves Lucifer. Lucifer was the beginning of His creation. God has been rejected and scorned. His name is used as a word for cursing rather than blessing by the rebellious angels and by many on earth. By others, His name is spoken out of fear rather than love. He has been horribly misunderstood and His character maligned. His pain is greater than you can imagine."

"I never thought about that," I said. "I know how excruciatingly painful it is to be rejected by my own children—by my own husband. Somehow, I never thought of God as having feelings. I pictured Him as a magnificent being sitting far away from His lowly creation."

Another silence while I absorbed what it must feel like for God to be rejected and maligned by those He loves and created. It was hard to think of God as being in pain, but then I remembered Jesus and what I knew about the pain that He experienced.

I switched my thoughts and finally said, "So, the universe has been watching earth and our experiment with sin to see who is right in this controversy. Has the haze lifted? Do heavenly beings understand it *all* now? Do they clearly know whether God or Lucifer is right?" I asked.

"Actually, we do not call Lucifer by his original name anymore," said Amor-el. "Instead of bearing light and knowledge about God as the name Lucifer signifies, he became God's opponent, sowing distrust and lies about

God. His name is now Satan which means 'accuser' or 'adversary.'"

Amor-el continued, "That partly answers your question, doesn't it? But let me answer your question more fully. Your world *has* unfolded in large part the mystery of sin to us. As you have correctly understood, earth has been the focal point of our attention since the inception of Satan's law of self-centeredness on your planet. The universe has watched closely to find out how selfish natures actually function—which gives us an insight as to who is correct in this controversy. But it was not until the cross that we fully understood the utter depravity of sin. But, Anne, you need a rest. This is a very intense experience for you."

I agreed that I needed a break. So we went for another little walk. The birds sang sweetly and there was perfume in the air. My, but I loved this place. But even more than the place, I loved the beings here.

CHAPTER FOUR

People Get Involved

Amor-el and I rested in a fragrant hammock made of living vines. As we swayed, the flowers in the vines gave out even more of their precious perfume. It was absolutely glorious. But despite the beauty, my mind was on fire with unanswered questions.

"I don't get it," I said. "Why did it take Jesus dying on the cross for you to be convinced? Couldn't you see the pitfalls of self-centeredness right away?"

"Not right away," said Amor-el. "There is an issue that on the one hand complicates matters, but on the other hand clears them up."

"Huh?" I questioned.

Amor-el continued, "After the rebellion began on earth, you experienced an environment that is in sharp contrast to heaven. After the rebellion, God granted to your first parents their desire—separation from the Spirit of God, from life. Of course, there is no death in heaven and no lack of anything. It was early understood in this controversy that only the experience of death and deprivation could efficiently and actually answer the questions Satan raised. Think of it this way. If the principle of self-sacrificing love is correct, it has to be correct in every situation—easy or stressful, and even in the face of death. Correct? A law is only good if it is *always* applicable."

I nodded my head in agreement.

Amor-el continued, "Thus, in God's great wisdom and respect for personal liberty, He allowed the alteration of conditions on earth. So your world, the earth, became the perfect environment to expose the true nature of sin. Heaven would be an inefficient place to bring a complete conclusion to the controversy between God and Satan. The environment of heaven is perfect—as you can see. But it made sense to us that principles by which we are to live need to be applicable whether there is physical ease or physical hardship, whether one experiences death or life. We also came to understand that whatever a being says, he or she only truly believes what he or she is willing to die for."

"You mean if we say that we love each other, but when we're facing starvation, we fight over the last piece of bread, we really don't love each other after all?" I queried.

"A good example," said Amor-el. "Only in a place where death is a reality and material necessities insufficient, could the principles of self-sacrificing love and selfishness truly be tested. We all agreed that death and suffering must be the test of Satan's principles *and* God's principles. Even though Satan claimed that in heaven, in a perfect environment and with uncompromised intellects, selfishness would not cause the problems that it does on earth. But then, because of the altered conditions on earth, Satan contended that man could not keep God's law perfectly, even were he to be imbued with God's Holy Spirit. So, Satan charged man's continued sinning on God. He stated that God and man would be eternally separated *unless* God changed His law to accommodate their selfishness. God explained that His law could *never* be changed, even to meet man in his unhappy condition. But most of the loyal angels began to understand that only the degree of suffering would be lessened under perfect heavenly conditions and that divisions and hatred were sure to come, even here in heaven, if we adopted Satan's law of self-centeredness. But we weren't totally certain. So we watched earth with intense interest. God told us it would all be explained as earth's history unfolded."

Amor-el continued, "All this is played out among humans—a few of whom adhere to God's ways but most to selfishness." I saw tears in Amor-el's eyes again, but he continued: "The universe has watched and continues to watch your world with intense interest. Adversity tests God's and Satan's character and it tests people."

"That makes sense," I said. "My understanding has been opened in a way that I never imagined possible. In my own past, during the times that I believed God existed, I always thought that God was angry at the world and that death and suffering were punishments. I even thought that the sacrifice of Jesus was because God took out His anger against sinful people on Jesus, at least that is what I was taught. The Father seemed like an absolute unreasonable ogre. I couldn't reconcile the character of Jesus with the mean-spirited nature of God, the way He was presented to me."

"That is typical human thinking. You have been tainted by the adversary," said Amor-el. "The sacrifice of Prince Michael was to reconcile *man* to God and not *God* to man. God doesn't punish the way you humans think of it. Every action of God toward the human race is redemptive—an attempt to re-establish love and to help you understand the necessity of respecting His great law of love, His law of self-sacrificing love. Every action on God's part is calculated to elevate and bring humanity back to the true understanding of Him. God has been unjustly accused of many things on earth. In reality, He has shown the utmost humility and fairness to all. He has allowed Himself to be thoroughly investigated by the universe. And we have found Him to be just and righteous, unselfish and merciful. But I know you don't understand all this yet. When you do, you will join us in thanking God. You will not hate Him for your suffering and the world's suffering."

"Pardon my bluntness," said Amor-el, "but in your present selfish condition, God had to create conditions that would help you understand your own self-centered nature, the harmfulness of selfishness and the deceptiveness of sin. A world where imminent death is a possibility and scarcity is a reality is the only world where you, in your selfishness, could understand how destructive the principle of selfishness really is. One of your leaders, Gandhi, rightly said, 'The world has enough for everyone's needs, but not enough for everyone's greed.' But God's thought is higher than Gandhi's. He gave

> *"One of your leaders, Gandhi, rightly said, 'The world has enough for everyone's needs, but not enough for everyone's greed.'"*

Himself unreservedly to meet man's understanding and draw man to Himself again."

"This controversy between God and Satan is coming into focus." I paused. "So, what do I have to do to come back to this wonderful place?"

Amor-el's face lit up with a joy that was impossible to hide. As my mind opened to these new truths, I realized that what I was learning had to be applied personally.

"God gives a time of probation to all people," said Amor-el. "His objective is not to disqualify anyone from eternity but to reconnect with whoever chooses to respond to His invitation and, of course, His purpose is also an eternal remedy for rebellion. You see, humans are born *without* the fullness of the Holy Spirit indwelling in them.

To see the completeness of the remedy, you will have to follow my reasoning closely. Your first parents rejected God's Spirit and joined Satan's side—so that, by nature, they consulted only themselves to decide what is good. But in mercy, God restored limited communion between the individual and Himself through the Holy Spirit. This communion opened the way for man to be *able* to choose restoration and reunion with Him. Without that partial restoration, man had nothing among which to choose. He was totally given to self-centeredness. You call the great gift of the Holy Spirit, conscience. One has to fight off the convictions of the Holy Spirit to be lost. Unfortunately, in your world's fallen condition, many do just that. They believe they are very good and have no need to listen to God's voice or to search for revelations about Him."

"So God restored in some measure the Holy Spirit to everyone?" I asked.

Amor-el continued, "Yes. Do you remember reading in the Bible that God put enmity between the woman and the serpent?[6] If God had not graciously restored the communication with mankind through a partial impartation of the Holy Spirit, no human would even be able to choose to return to God. In heaven, it took a conscious decision by the rebellious to expel God's Spirit, but once the principle of selfishness has taken hold in a person's mind, which is your human inheritance, it takes a conscious decision to desire God's Spirit and allow Him to fight against your very nature, to restore and to purify you. The fight against the sinful nature invites more and more of the Holy Spirit to indwell. This only happens by the human responding positively to God's Spirit. You call it repentance, confession, and spiritual growth. Because by nature man is now self-centered, he could *never* by himself even imagine the concept of being sacrificially loving to anyone. God's Spirit is a gift from God. The Spirit, speaking gently to one, reminds a person about the things heard about God and pleads for a response to love. Yes, without the Holy Spirit's work for each one, there would be no hope for restoration. Some people listen to God's Spirit and respond; many don't."

In a subdued voice, I said, "Truly, God's Spirit speaks to everyone—Christian and non-Christian—doesn't He? I have heard His voice even when I considered myself agnostic."

"Those that hear His voice and respond are His," said Amor-el. "There are many around the world who have *not* been privileged to learn about our blessed Prince Michael, but they listen to the Spirit's voice and respond. You would be surprised to see who they are! And many professed followers of God are not His at all. Consider what you know about the Inquisition and the Crusades— evil disgustingly done in God's name but inspired by the adversary. God's mercy and salvation from selfishness does not reach only those that have heard some sort of 'special' message. God is fair to all His creatures. Consequently, people are only responsible for the spiritual light they have been exposed to and are able to understand. Then they are judged as to whether they accept or reject it. It is the test for all humans."

"Got it," I said rather flippantly but felt humbled. I used to hate God for the Crusades and the Inquisition. Then in a serious tone, I said, "It seems fair that humans would be tested by their response to God's Spirit, and it would be fair for God to reach all people in some way. And I can understand that the remedy for rebellion is the indwelling by God's Spirit. But you said something very strange earlier. You said that *God Himself* was—or is— being investigated and tested by adversity?"

"Yes. God has allowed Himself to be thoroughly investigated—and tested. That is correct," said Amor-el.

"I might be able to understand that God could be investigated, but how can God be tested?" I half-grinned, almost triumphantly, at my own intelligence.

"Do you remember Satan's charge that God is selfish? God warned us that death would be the outcome of rebellion," said Amor-el.

"Yes," I said.

"Satan charged that God could not be touched with danger and that He lived in continuous safety, while Satan stood the risk of dying for his lofty ideas in order to benefit all creation. God had an answer to that accusation—a perfect answer. At the appointed time, Prince Michael would live on earth as a human being. We were awestruck, and frankly terrified, when that promise was given to humans—that Prince Michael would come and share the humanity of your people. Consider the magnificence of Prince Michael who created the perfection of the universe and whom angels adore. Then consider your low, fallen natures. It is totally astonishing that He became one with you. But, most of all, we understood perfectly that as one of you, He *could* be subject to death. *Now* God Himself could be tested through the Prince. Now He was God in human flesh. The universe watched with intense interest the life of Prince Michael on earth—God in human flesh. What would He be like in that wretched place? We feared that He would succumb to self-centeredness under the dire circumstances that we saw on earth, and we weren't sure what it would mean for the heavenly host."

I must have seemed unmoved to Amor-el. He shook his head and looked at me intensely, "You truly cannot understand." He looked at me again. "You haven't seen the true glory of Prince Michael. The angels bow in reverence to Him. We praised Him continually for the life that we borrow from Him. He paused again. "We saw Him create worlds, from the vast oceans to the majestic mountains, from the giant creatures to the tiniest perfect forms of life, creating systems of harmonious life and we sang for joy. Can you understand?"

"I think so." I tried to imagine Jesus creating these magnificent angel beings. I imagined Him creating microbes, birds, bugs, plants, animals, and people.

Amor-el continued: "To our surprise, Jesus wasn't born to a high-ranking family but to a hard-working common woman who loved God as much as she was capable of. His adoptive father was also of the same kind." Amor-el paused for a moment. "And yet, by humiliating Himself, Jesus revealed God's character more fully to us and in ways that we could never, never understand before. Through His redemption of humanity, He is dearer and more glorious in our sight than He was before He became human."

Amor-el continued, "The battle between Prince Michael and Satan was great in heaven but it intensified more so on earth. Satan was relentless against the Prince. The Adversary claimed that he was in control of the entire world and that he now owned it and all its beings—and it was true. Except when our Prince Michael came to your world, Satan's claim was no longer true. Satan did not own the *entire* world. Even in childhood, by His perfect obedience, Prince Michael—Jesus—started dispelling Satan's lies about God's character. Jesus came to you to communicate, as one of you, the loving, healing nature of God. God rightfully called Him Jesus—'Jehovah is Savior.' Jesus shared in your humanity while Satan pursued Him at every step of His life on earth attempting to push Him, prod Him and force Him to distrust God. Jesus came to earth to magnify God's law. He gave us greater insights into God's law of self-sacrificing love by demonstrating that God loves His beings not just to the *point* of death but into death itself."

I looked puzzled and Amor-el stopped speaking. He waited for me to speak, sensing my confusion.

"The more I learn, the more questions I have," I mused. "Isn't Jesus actually God? How could He have shared totally in humanity? He couldn't have felt everything that I do. He couldn't have been tempted like I am."

"It's hard to think of God in that manner, isn't it?" said Amor-el with a winsome smile. "But Jesus had a human mother and received from her a human inheritance with all the physical, mental, and moral destruction that sin has wrought through the years. If it had been other than that, Satan would have objected because Jesus would not have been a true human being and the loyal beings, and humanity, would not have had a satisfactory answer to Satan's accusations that man *cannot* obey the law of God. If Jesus did not have man's nature, He would be lifted above the temptations of mankind and His sacrifice would have been meaningless unless you believe erroneously that God took out His wrath about sin against Jesus. Then when His anger was quenched, He was able to forgive human beings. There is nowhere in Scripture to support such an illogical conclusion."

A light came on in my mind. "So, when Jesus said in the Garden of Gethsemane, '[N]ot my will, but thine' (Luke 22:42), He really meant it? It wasn't just some nice words to placate God?" I questioned. "It was as difficult for Him to yield to God's will at that time as it is for me now?"

"I need to explain more fully," said Amor-el. "Though fully a man, with all of man's thinking patterns inherited from Mary and inheriting the physical debilities of His ancestry, He was a man fully indwelled by the Holy Spirit. To succeed where Adam had failed and to become the link between the Father and man, Jesus laid down His divine power, His omniscience, and His physical majesty, becoming obedient to God's will for Him as the Father unfolded it to Him day by day. Unlike other humans, Jesus had a perfect understanding of God's character because He was indwelled by the Holy Spirit but still subject to man's temptations. You have to remember that your first parents were also indwelled by the Spirit and gave in to temptations. For that matter, the fallen angels were indwelled by the Spirit."

I thought about Jesus' ancestry for a minute. I remembered some of them from Bible class—Rahab, a harlot;[7] David, who was a liar, adulterer, and a murderer;[8] and a line of derelict kings. But then a thought came to my mind, *But then there was Jesus' divinity.* "So, He was *not* tempted like I am?" I asked.

"Actually, He was tempted beyond your temptations because His trials were much more difficult than yours. But the principle entrenched in His temptations was the same— Jesus needed to have total trust in God in every particular. Satan pressed Jesus ferociously to give up His trust in the Father. God allowed Satan to press Jesus in a stronger way than He did Adam and Eve," said Amor-el. "Your first parents could only be tempted by contact with Satan at the forbidden tree of the knowledge of good and evil. Jesus was hounded continually—as is all mankind now."

Amor-el continued, "You, Anne, fail on the smallest points. Jesus was pushed to the limits of endurance. During His life, He was utterly humiliated—both physically and mentally. Satan took the opportunity of His physical weakness to pose before Him the temptation to disobey the will of the Father and to do what was more pleasing to His human nature—thereby distrusting God. He was tempted to use His powers to benefit Himself. After a forty-day fast in the desert,[9] Jesus was tempted to feed Himself and not rely on His Father providing for Him. Even though His Father had directed Him to go to the desert, He had provided not a speck of food for forty days. On the cross, Jesus was tempted to perform a miracle on His own behalf to save His life and to convince the people that He *is* their Messiah instead of relying on His Father's provision and relying on His Father's plan for salvation."

"I am beginning to see," I said. "The slightest distrust of God, the slightest use of power for His own benefit would have been the same as eating from the tree of the knowledge of good and evil had been for our first parents. He would have questioned God's right to define good and evil. He would have agreed with Satan's position that God cannot be trusted and that creatures know what is best for themselves. Anything outside of God's will would have meant distrust of God, and by His actions, Jesus would be agreeing with Satan that God cannot be trusted. I guess that means that He would have pushed out the Holy Spirit from His life. He would have acknowledged that people cannot keep God's law of self-sacrificing love." I was humbled. "It is more amazing than I ever thought. I am totally floored that Jesus didn't give in to Satan in the least."

"Your thoughts and conclusion are correct. Precisely. As I said before," continued Amor-el with another of his winsome smiles, "even though encumbered with humanity, Jesus understood the character of God intimately. Had He distrusted God, He would have done so with the full knowledge of God's character. Satan would have triumphantly prevailed in the controversy."

"Oh, I think I understand. So, when Jesus was baptized, He wasn't just putting on an act," I said. "I always wondered why a perfect person needed to be baptized. I guess the baptism meant that He was acknowledging his day-by-day choice to die to His human inheritance, His human nature. Could I even say 'sinful' nature?"

"Yes," said Amor-el. "Human nature is sinful and it was Jesus' inheritance, but in all this, He did not sin. Sinful nature does not necessarily make a sinning individual, as we see in the life of Jesus. In as much as human nature is 'sinful,' or has a natural bent toward self-centeredness, Jesus struggled with His humanity, but love for His Father and admiration of His Father's loving character motivated Jesus' obedience. He struggled against His humanity but gave Himself totally to God in every particular and the universe found Him perfect in every respect. Indeed, when He struggled in the garden, saying, '[N]ot my will, but thine, be done' (Luke 22:42), His human nature shrank from the trial to which the situation impelled Him and to which God was allowing Him to go. But He chose to submit His human nature to God and *not* to do what was more pleasing to Himself as a human."

"Not that I have done it very often, but struggling against sin is not easy," I said with a chuckle and then added seriously, "There are people who have hurt me tremendously and to be able to eradicate enemies with just a thought would be an overwhelming temptation. I'll bet you angels can't really understand what Jesus went through."

"We have followed individual lives closely and have seen sin's effects," Amor-el responded, "but you are right, the loyal angels cannot totally understand sin. Only Jesus can truly understand the power of self-centeredness because He overcame it. As a man, where your first parents and all their progeny miserably failed, Jesus did not."

I paused speaking to allow these new thoughts to sink in, then I continued, "So, God was tested through Jesus. *And* humanity, infused with the Holy Spirit, was tested through Jesus. He was like a super second Adam who did not fail in His obedience to God." I paused. "He was like a second Adam but with a sinful human inheritance. And He is God. I see how God was tested."

"You must always remember," said Amor-el, "your salvation does not benefit humanity alone. It is for the entire universe. Your struggles allow us to understand that, in the end sin, the principle of selfishness, living without God's Holy Spirit, destroys itself—it is an untenable way to organize life. Satan told us that his way would elevate us. But it hasn't done that for you humans. You humans fight with each other continually. You strive for supremacy; you hurt and destroy when you do not get your own way."

> *"You strive for supremacy; you hurt and destroy when you do not get your own way."*

I inhaled deeply. I saw myself only too vividly portrayed. Then a question popped into my mind, "So, if Satan's ideas in heaven were initially presented as doing good to others, why couldn't angels in heaven see that Satan was doing the evil on earth and end this controversy? I mean, Satan in heaven didn't encourage the angels to lie, steal, cheat, and hurt each other when he started this whole mess, did he? Why is he doing that on earth?"

"Well, the best way to explain that is that when one is trying to topple a tyrant on earth—someone who is hurting many, many people—it seems a wicked thing not to use *any* means available to bring about justice. Would you agree?"

"I guess so," I said.

"You guessed correctly," said Amor-el.

"Consequently, Satan felt that there should be no limits to his strategy. Lying was not a problem. He said that God lies too. This is how Satan presented his strategy to us and to his angels, but he knew God's character better than that—God is upright in every respect. Jesus said that Satan was a liar from the beginning. Satan was not honest. If he didn't sin knowingly, it wouldn't be sin. In answer to your other question about Satan's motivation to get people to behave in disgusting ways, ways that he didn't advocate in heaven, the answer is rather simple. Satan knows that God intensely abhors sin and suffering. If he could make mankind so disgusting to God, perhaps God would rise up and even He would gently destroy all the inhabitants of the earth. The earth's multitudes honor greed, wealth, and power rather than goodness and mercy. Moral corruption is seen as a virtue. There is hatred all around. The loyal angels had all seen enough. Indeed, *we* watched for God to rise up in indignation and sweep away all the inhabitants of the earth and end the misery once and for all. We would have totally understood the necessity. But then Satan would blame God for causing death and destruction on earth. Satan would be free from blame and exult that he had proved his point: that it is impossible for people, just as it is for God, to always follow the principle of self-sacrificing love and that self-centeredness in a perfect environment is what is called for."

Amor-el continued, "In order to understand Satan's strategy, you must remember that there are only two possible laws in the universe: God's law of self-sacrificing love and Satan's law of self-centeredness. Satan doesn't have to prove that his law is superior, he just has to prove that God's law doesn't work in all circumstances. If God's law doesn't work in all circumstances, then by default, Satan's principle would be true."

"Oh. Of course. That's why Satan tried so hard to subvert Jesus. Because there are only the two underlying principles possible—self-sacrificing love and self-centeredness, disestablishing God's principle in Jesus would automatically prove his own," Amor-el smiled in approval. I had understood.

Then in pursuit of understanding, even though I risked losing Amor-el's smile of approval, I said, "Well, maybe Satan has a point." I pushed on: "People can't follow God's law of self-sacrificing love on earth. If we hadn't seen the example of Jesus, we wouldn't even understand that such a thing as self-sacrificing love existed. On earth, we're all just trying to survive and protect our families. We are really just struggling and trying to come out better in life." Amor-el raised an eyebrow. It seemed as though he read my thoughts. I continued, "Well, maybe if we do better it means that someone else isn't doing so well, but … that's just the way that it is. We just can't follow God's law on earth. It's just too hard."

"Indeed. It is hard. Indeed, you can't. But God had a better way. He sent His Son to give the world hope and to explain, by His life, the true character of God. Some would love Jesus and desire His Spirit."

I remained in silent thought for a few moments. God's response to a world bent on evil and directed by Satan was to send Jesus as a helpless baby, to grow into a man with a perfect life to rescue those who would follow Him. "It's true, Jesus made the world a better place. He *did* change the course of history," I admitted. "The first Christians *were* truly loving people even in the face of intense persecution." My defenses were being broken down. I felt myself giving my mind over to Jesus. But then a thought came to me that needed expression.

CHAPTER FIVE

More Confusion

"OK. So, I need to stop and ask a question," I said. "You know that the Bible is an accurate history of the earth, right? I mean, you've actually seen it all happen."

"Of course," answered Amor-el. "God has seen to it that people in your time period have an accurate witness to the truth."[10]

"Then if God is love, why did He kill everyone in the flood, including babies?" I asked.

Amor-el frowned. "God, it appears, is always the first to be blamed in a catastrophe." Amor-el sighed, pausing for a few seconds. "But consider what is happening in your world today. Is God to blame for the wars, rapes, thefts, and injustice? Hardly. Here, let me explain step by step. The first thing to understand is that God has the power to be in absolute control of everything. Isn't that so?"

"Yes," I agreed. "But isn't it true that God refuses to lie or use force?"

"That is so true," said Amor-el. "You understand." He smiled at me. I was proud of myself for understanding at least that. Amor-el continued, "But God has *allowed* certain things to take place that are not according to His will, such as the current rebellion against Him which causes terror, oppression, and disaster, agreed?"

"It appears so," I agreed again.

"So, you will find it written in the Bible, which is the guidebook for humans, that God assumes responsibility for everything because everything is in His power. The evil that He does not stop, He assumes responsibility for, even though He was not the cause of it,"[11] said Amor-el.

"OK. That makes sense." I paused and then said, "So, God didn't cause the flood?"

"Have you considered that the flood might have been the natural result of the greed of the people living before the flood?"[12] said Amor-el.

"Their own greed? No, I don't understand," I said.

"Your education has taught you that man, beginning in a primitive position, is getting better and better but, in reality, man was created perfect and the individual is degenerating. Before the flood, there were people of much greater physical strength and intellectual achievement than in your generation.[13] They lived hundreds of years and added to their store of knowledge daily. Steady gains after the Reformation have allowed your society to again reach a point where it can make great engineering strides but only based on the work of previous generations. The pre-flood population worked the earth to their advantage but also to their destruction. God allowed them to destroy the delicate balance of the earth systems that He put into place," said Amor-el. "It's amazing that people think themselves smarter than God and deign to tamper with His creation."

"Are you saying that those people brought the flood on themselves?" I asked incredulously.

"Are you astounded that the people before the flood had power to destroy themselves?" asked Amor-el. "Look at your own generation. In only 100 years, your weak generation has moved from simple engineering inventions to highly polluting ones and to the ability to annihilate every person on earth. In Noah's day, God warned the inhabitants of the earth about the coming flood, but only Noah and his family believed God and were obedient to God's word. There are warning voices again today, but men are paralyzed by greed," said Amor-el passionately.

"Well, I agree we certainly are capable of destroying the earth," I said, thinking about the world's nuclear arsenals, the nuclear accidents, and the near nuclear accidents—not to mention pollution and the latest horrifying military technologies. "It's really amazing that so much of our energy goes into figuring out ways to destroy rather than to help each other. You know we just accept this kind of thinking as normal." I paused thinking about how messed up the world is and then continued with my questions: "OK. So maybe God didn't destroy the earth with a flood, maybe He just allowed it and rescued those obedient to Him. But He did order the Israelites to butcher women and children when they entered the Promised Land, didn't He? That is one reason I always had trouble believing that God is a God of love. The record makes it appear that He is harsh, severe, unforgiving, and even picks 'favorites.' Those stories filled me with fear because it seemed only a flick of fate could have put me in the group of destroyed persons. Those unfortunate people had no control over where they were born." I wondered how Amor-el was going to make sense of that mystery. I hoped he was not going to be offended by my forthright questions, but, as usual, I had no reason to fear.

"It is confusing, is it not?" said Amor-el. "Let me explain it this way. But first, let me assure you that God makes all things fair in the end, even though it may not seem so to you at times. My reasoning may seem a little contorted, but you will understand in the end." He paused and then continued, "Anne, let me take you back to God's original design for mankind and then compare the present situation of the world. It will help you understand.

God's original design bound all creation to Him by His Holy Spirit. The Spirit spoke directly to all men. All were obedient to God because they trusted and loved Him. The fruit of their obedience was supreme love toward God and lavish love toward each other. There was harmony, health, and pleasures physical, intellectual, and spiritual. God's law of love reigned supreme."

"On earth, Adam and Eve," continued Amor-el "rejected God by believing Satan. By eating the forbidden fruit, they agreed with Satan that God could not be trusted. Deliberately severing their trust relationship with God, Adam and Eve lost the blessed presence of the Holy Spirit. Men became subject to a slavery more terrible than physical slavery—a slavery to self that makes a person's greatest ambition that of serving himself. Here, let me diagram it for you." He began to write in the air and the writing was visible. Wow! By this time, I just learned to accept such things. "In God's plan, He is the great center, and everyone is connected with Him through the Spirit." Amor-el drew a circle with God's name in it. Then he drew little people connected to God by flames representing the Holy Spirit. Then, on another section of his tablet, Amor-el drew a throne and upon it sat a huge letter "I." "This," said Amor-el, "is your present condition and the condition of the world. With everyone serving himself, the only way to survive together is for men to institute laws. But laws are not effective without punishment. So, the big 'I' paradigm only works when a system of laws and punishment is set up. In fortunate circumstances, laws are instituted through a more democratic process, but often laws are written by a dictator, or a ruling class, who rule with complete coercive power. Great darkness came upon the earth when allegiance shifted from God's perfect rule to the big 'I' model. Those more physically or intellectually imposing rule over others. On an everyday level, many families are ruled in this despotic way."

I remembered my ex-husband and nodded my head.

"Contrast that, Anne, with God's gentle manner of governance," said Amor-el. "God's Spirit of love ruled in everyone's mind."

"I guess there is no need for a police force in heaven," I chuckled.

"None at all," said Amor-el. "But remember that God's law is unflinching—every precept must be perfectly obeyed or there can be no peace. Not because God is a despot but because God's law is the unwavering truth."

Amor-el continued, "God was grieved at the situation. His mercy and love desired to give man the ability to reconnect with Him. In the garden—just after sin—God restored, in some measure, the gift of the Holy Spirit. He promised to put hatred between the woman and the serpent (Gen. 3:15). Think of it, your first parents had just given themselves totally to Satan and his principle of self-centeredness. Without a partial restoration of the Holy Spirit, there could be *only* harmony between mankind and Satan, consequently no choice. God restored choice to mankind through the Holy Spirit. But, as you yourself know, some people live by God's Spirit but most don't. God's desire for man's salvation is hampered by the unbelief of earthlings and their fear of God instilled in them by Satan and man's now natural bent toward autonomy, sin. God could not work in ways that He wanted to work among the people on earth. Thus, we see some of the strange things that God did or seems to have done in trying to re-establish relationship with the people on earth. God is always limited by man's unbelief. God wanted to bring the Israelites into the Promised Land by using hornets[14] to carve out a living space for the Israelites in Canaan but He could not because of their lack of faith in Him. God intended to have a people through which the Prince could come. His intention was that His people would have faith in Him alone and He would bring them into the land of Canaan the way that they started their journey—with no weapons but by miracles alone. Instead, the move into Palestine was done by force of arms but that was not God's preference. Canaan was a wide place with few inhabitants and room for everyone. God was going to plant His people there to become a nation ruled by His divine precepts and it would become a magnet for the righteous. At the time of their entry into Canaan, Egypt had an overbearing presence in the land of Canaan. When the Canaanites realized that this small group of people destroyed the Egyptian army—not by strength of numbers or the might of their army but because of their faith in God—they were awed. They heard about God's miracles in Egypt, the parting of the Red Sea and the drowning of Pharaoh's elite army. They heard about the manna, the laws protecting the innocent and women, the Ten Commandments, the wise civil laws, and an open invitation to join God's people. But it didn't sway most of them. The Gibeonites were an exception (Josh. 9:3–27). The Canaanites continued in their disgusting sexual rites, often sacrificing people and even their own children to their cruel gods."

"God," Amor-el continued, "has always established a relationship with those who sought Him. Notable was Abraham, Moses, and many, many others. God heard their plea to protect them from harm and especially to use them to disseminate knowledge about Him. Early on, God provided the written Word as a bridge to re-establishing relationship and as a testimony of His will so that no one could easily alter His Word—it was memorialized in writing."

"Sometimes God's dealings with people seem harsh," continued Amor-el. "Sometimes His actions seem harsh because God allows sin to take its course. We find Him majorly hampered by the unbelief of those who should have been more closely guided by His Spirit. Satan worked diligently to denigrate the Jewish people. On the one hand, he moved on the people to accept pagan practices and on the other hand, he moved on some to accept a form of religion that did not really love God and their neighbor as themselves. Satan is always working to deceive mankind. He encourages them to believe that God will accept them in their sins or that they can become righteous by developing their own goodness—that they can be righteous toward God but ignore and even be cruel to those around them and still be in favor with God. Finally, when Jesus came to earth and re-established an untainted relationship with people, there was phenomenal spiritual growth among some of mankind. When people adhered to God's principles, society flourished. When they did not adhere, society waned. But returning to God does not mean that it is enough to design society using *some* of God's principles. Using only *some* of God's principles means that people continue in the law/punishment—the grand 'I' mode. God, for the good of mankind, wants to reconnect by His original design—as on the day of Pentecost when the Holy Spirit came down on His people in great power (Acts 2)."

Amor-el continued, "The human experiment with sin has convinced heavenly beings that the only reasonable, loving way to govern is by God's original design. Anne, let God's aim of reconnection and the character of Jesus be the prism through which you understand the Holy Scriptures. Some have interpreted Scriptures to mean that violence in the pursuit of spiritual uniformity is acceptable to God. It is not. Consider the great law of God, the Ten Commandments, condemning murder, and consider the character of Jesus renouncing all violence, and let that be your guide. After the coming of Jesus and His direct command to love one another, any type of violence is precluded. The aim of God's people is to save, not destroy."

"But the world doesn't really live that way," I said. "You mean that we should get rid of the police?"

"Surely not," said Amor-el. "If the whole world were connected to God by His Spirit, no police would be needed. But the world is not ordered according to God's original design and there must be civil authority for the protection of the innocent."

"Amor-el, we haven't discussed war, but I think I get it. As far as I am concerned, I have the answer to a question I have really wondered about for a long time. I could never kill anyone, and now as a believer in God's love, my mission is to save life and help people reconnect with God and become part of His kingdom. You know, I feel sorry for the destruction of these ancient people, but then I look at people today and get totally disgusted. Our greatest inventions are used to destroy one another. Airplanes are used to drop bombs. Knowledge about the atom is turned into making bigger and more destructive bombs. People terrorize for political power, killing the innocent. Tobacco executives sell their poison hoping to enslave as many people as possible. We are totally disgusting. It must be hard to watch," I said.

> *"As far as I am concerned, I have the answer to a question I have really wondered about for a long time."*

"We endure the pain of watching in the hope of reconnecting with some," Amor-el said wistfully.

Then Amor-el motioned for me to get closer. "God wants me to help you understand some of the battles that Jesus fought for you." He paused slightly, then continued, "The first battle on earth between God's law of love and the principle of selfishness was lost in the Garden of God—in Eden—when Adam failed to trust His benevolent Creator. But the war was won in another garden. Look, the Son is struggling with an almost overwhelming temptation in the garden."

"Please, please, before we go to the garden, please tell me something. I have never understood it so that it made sense to me. How does Jesus' death save *me*? I've heard all the trite phrases: 'saved by the blood,' 'Jesus died for our sins,' but I don't really know what it means. I told you already that at one time it seemed to me that God was angry about sin, and He took out His anger on Jesus, so that then He wasn't so angry anymore and then we were free from God's anger. But really that never made sense to me, and it certainly contradicts what I have been learning here in this beautiful place. Anyway, in terms of an all-knowing God, how can He accept the life of an innocent person dying for the guilty? Even the legal system of sinful mankind doesn't allow for such an injustice. But, if I am beginning to put this puzzle together correctly, the death of Jesus was not to pay a penalty of some type but to show the true nature of the sin that is in our minds—that inward sin, carried to its conclusion, would cause the rebellious creature to destroy even his own Creator if he had the chance. I am starting to see that *God* did not kill Jesus in some sort of fiendish, vindictive way, but God allowed evil men to put Jesus to death. But how, I still don't understand how Jesus' death saves *me*? Can you help me understand?"

"I was expecting you to ask me that," said Amor-el. "Certainly, I will explain. First, there is a most important point that humans have lost sight of. Let me explain it in this way. You agree, I'm sure, that there is a commonality in human nature which makes you all rather predictable. In our observations of humans, we angels always knew what a sinful person would do, given a certain set of circumstances—he would act selfishly—in what he considered to be his own best interests. Often the more stressful the situation, the more grievous the sinful act. There is no end to this cycle. The conclusion can be drawn that sinful nature causes a man, unchecked by God's Spirit, to be capable of *any* sin however heinous. What do you think?"

"Well, I guess so," I said.

"You don't need to guess. Given the proper situation and timing there is *no* sin of which any of you are incapable. Unless submitted to God's Spirit, the ungodly work hard to do what is socially acceptable but the motivation is the same—self-centeredness. You do a helpful act in hopes of a reward, whether the rewarder is God or human society. Remember that, by nature, no one person is better than any other. Murder, theft, lying—any sin—are all the results of not allowing the Holy Spirit to direct the life. Sin is a mindset that is in opposition to God. Therefore, there is no 'small' sin. Jesus taught you that. In its essence, hatred is the same as murder, lust the same as adultery, and coveting the same as theft. Sin is a rejection of the Holy Spirit, and it leads to acting in sinful ways. Until converted to God's way, you all act under the big 'I' mode."

"Well, I never thought of it, but I guess …. No. It *is* true—that if I had been born into a different situation, to different parents, if I lived under difficult circumstances, I could easily imagine myself participating in any sin. I admit that my mindset is sinful," I grinned uncomfortably. "That doesn't say much for humans, does it?"

"No. But it doesn't say much for *any* created being. The universe understands now that creatures, uninhabited by the Holy Spirit are capable of any sin—even angels. Consider what happened to the exalted Lucifer and his followers. But, on the contrary, the life of Jesus shows that even a man subjected to the degenerating physical effects of 4,000 years of sin, if he is imbued with the Holy Spirit, is capable of obedience to God's law, to perfect love. Though Jesus was tempted to the utmost, He never sinned. Therefore, man can overcome his sinful nature by the indwelling of the Holy Spirit. A thorough knowledge of God's true character engenders love for God, creates a true obedience and a genuine love for others. Yielding to the indwelling of the Holy Spirit directs the life in the path of obedience through a reconnection with God."

I looked at the pristine beauty around me—all nature in subjection to God, all beings in loving subjection to God, loving those around them. I longed to live in this place, and I longed for my children and others to live in this place. But I knew they would have to desire to be restored to the image of God.

"So, Jesus represents a humanity that has been restored to God! Oh, wow! The second Adam—perfect, unfallen." My eyes misted up, "If the whole world were filled with people like Jesus, in subjection to the will of God, voila—no more fear, only perfect peace."

"Yes."

I continued, "So Jesus did not die 'instead' of man, like being punished for our sins. He died 'as' a man—a man full of God's Holy Spirit—an example of what a human being, yielded totally to God can become. That potentially means even me! That's why Jesus' death can save me. I get it!"

"Yes. Exactly," said Amor-el. "The death of Jesus 'as' man's representative opened the gates of heaven to those who love Him, desire to follow Him, and want to become like Him."

"Oh, but I don't think I can ever really be like Jesus," I said.

"Do you *want* to be like Him?" asked Amor-el.

"Yes, I do now. Now that I am beginning to truly know what He is like," I said.

"God, in His own time, by your submission to Him, by desiring His Holy Spirit, will draw you closer and closer to Himself. Be patient. And be obedient. And continue to grow in your love for God. Cling to Him," said Amor-el. "Your faith in Jesus saves you. You are saved by His blood—the symbol of His life."

"I desire all of that," I whispered. But I knew Amor-el heard me.

Amor-el spoke triumphantly, "We will never exhaust our growth in adoring God and becoming more like Him. And still, eternity will beckon us on to more and more of His likeness."

Jesus

Now with a deeper insight, I desired to see what Amor-el wanted to show me. I sighed audibly. "I am ready to go back to the garden," I said. "I want to see Jesus."

I searched the scene. "Which one is He? How can I tell who He is?" I asked.

"He is the One who is a little taller than the other three with Him," said Amor-el.

"Oh, yes," I said. "I see Him walking away from the others to be by Himself."

Amor-el continued, "All through His life on earth, Jesus was pained by the self-centeredness of those around Him. But He ever gave of Himself. He was misunderstood, ridiculed, and hated for it almost without exception. He worked diligently to alleviate the suffering of those hurt by sin. He found joy in healing, but at the same time, He Himself was daily wounded by His interactions with sinful, ungrateful people."

Amor-el's noble face grew exceedingly tense. "Now Jesus is facing the culmination of the hatred that He has experienced from childhood. For three-and-a-half years, He taught Israel about the loving character of God, the need to follow God's law of love, the need to seek an infilling of the Holy Spirit, and His teachings were confirmed by miracles of healing. In return, the leaders of Israel furiously hated Him and deceptively planned His murder. The rich and powerful knew that if the people followed Him, their hold on the nation would be broken and the leaders would lose their personal exalted place in society. Even though Jesus was as a chain let down from heaven, drawing men upward to God, He knew that He was to be murdered because men would not submit to God and love one another," said Amor-el. "The cross is sinful man's response to God's love. He has borne your griefs and your sorrows. He has made Himself an offering on the altar of your sin."[15]

"An offering for sin?" I asked. "You don't mean an offering to God? I thought I understood you to say that God didn't take out His anger on Jesus in order to be able to pardon us from sin."

"Of course," said Amor-el. "God doesn't need a blood offering to forgive sin." Amor-el's voice softened. "The offering was for you. And for me. Without Jesus' life and His death at the hands of sin and sinners, we would not understand the true nature of sin, and Satan's accusations could not be refuted. The offering was for us. God ordained it for our benefit because there was no other way for us to understand the nature of sin and the extent of His great love. Satan had stated that no one could keep God's law of love but here was One who did. And men's response? 'Kill Him.' 'Get Him away from us.' 'We will not have this Man to rule over us' (Luke 19:14, paraphrase)."

I thought of the many times that I had those thoughts, the many times I had rebuffed those trying to tell me about Jesus, the many times I ignored His voice. Extreme sorrow took hold of me, and I wept. Through my tears, I turned my attention again to the garden. I saw a number of olive trees. A human figure clung to the ground. I could just barely see the side of His face. His face glistened with sweat even though the air was cool. A strained and desperate voice cried out, 'Father, not my will but Thine be done. Oh, Father let this cup pass from Me. But if I must drink it, Thy will be done' (Luke 22:42, paraphrase)."

There was nothing with which I could compare the desperation in His voice. He spoke with such intensity. His body clung to the ground.

"The Father and the Prince Jesus have always been as One," Amor-el whispered in reverent awe. "Even closer than the closest earthly father and son, closer than any husband and wife, closer than mother and child. During His life on earth, Jesus felt His Father's continual approval. He felt the Father's presence—always. He felt His protection and love. When rejected by people, even His closest whom He loved so intensely, Jesus gained comfort from His Father. He constantly requested power from God to work on behalf of men. But now Jesus knows He will be put into the hands of sinful men—men inspired by Satan—who will inflict excruciating pain and humiliation on His body and upon His mind. But more so, through the inspiration of Satan, men will try to drive Him to the point of forsaking His trust in

> *There was nothing with which I could compare the desperation in His voice. He spoke with such intensity. His body clung to the ground.*

God's love. So, the onslaught will be intense, unrelenting. His humanity shrinks from the combat with Satan and his agents. Jesus hopes that God will intervene, but He knows that the Scripture says that God will step aside and allow Him to be tested to the utmost—even to death (Isa. 52:14–15, 53:1-12; Zech. 13:7; Heb. 5:8). The awful temptation in the wilderness was but a faint precursor to this temptation.

The mental agony outweighs the physical agony. Judas, whom Jesus loves intensely, will betray Him. His disciples, whom He loves without reservation, will abandon Him. His Father will leave Him to cruel hands to fulfill His ultimate will of saving mankind. *And* He knows that it is within His own ability to save Himself from this physical and mental torture. He is tempted to wonder whether His death will really be fruitful. He has sacrificed so much already just to be on earth. He longs to flee to His Father and stand innocent, as He truly is, before Him. But if He does that, He knows that mankind is doomed to eternal separation from God—death with no hope. Other than Him, they have no way for redemption from the plague of evil self-centeredness and the cruel and deceptive rule of Satan. Even though the people around Jesus are ignorant of it, their eternal destiny is in His hands. What He is doing will open heaven to them or leave them with no hope. Through this last struggle, He has no earthly support. He is alone. All alone. And He only senses the presence of God *by faith* in Their previous closeness and in the knowledge of the exalted, loving character of God. But He *feels* utterly and totally rejected as He is allowed to fall under the control of Satan working through sinful men and then to sink into what is, to all appearances, the total annihilation of death with no hope of a resurrection—except by faith which feels impossible to Him. Because He is so closely associated with sinful mankind, He fears there will be no resurrection from the dead for Him. He fears nothing will have been accomplished for mankind, but *He* will be eternally extinguished in His attempt to save mankind. Satan whispers these thoughts to Jesus. But He rejects all of Satan's thoughts and pushes on by faith in God's Word even though it all looks very disastrous to Him."

Amor-el and I watched as Jesus was taken from the garden to the unlawful trials in front of the Sanhedrin,

Pilate, and Herod. We saw the slaps, the spitting, and the derision. It was repulsive, yet I kept watching, unable to look away. Then the whip cut again and again into His already scored and bleeding flesh. The barbaric soldiers pushed a crown of thorns onto His head and laughed when blood flowed down His head and onto His beard and dripped on the ground. The cruel soldiers made fun of Him in the most obscene, humiliating, and invasive ways. Finally, they forced Him to carry the heavy cross while they poked and prodded Him as though He were an animal. At Calvary, they stripped Him totally naked, nailed His hands and feet to the cross. It was a sickening, disgusting sight. I saw the raw flesh, the blood dripping, and heard the screams and shrieking of those around Him.

I had never understood the extent of the emotional and physical suffering that Jesus endured. Yet, amazingly, He had only gentle, loving words for His torturers. Even then you could see on His face that He loved them. Instead of hating them, Jesus pitied them for what they were doing. A crown of thorns was thrust onto His head. I remembered that thorns had appeared on earth after sin entered, not before. The crown of thorns meant by the soldiers as an insult was a fitting symbol of a kingdom gone awry, captured by Satan.

I was sickened and horrified but utterly amazed as I looked at Jesus' face. I had never before seen such profound love in the presence of such overwhelming hatred. Hoping that Jesus was comforted in some way, I asked my companion, "Jesus *knew* that He would be resurrected. He kept telling everyone that. Didn't He know what would happen? Wasn't He comforted by that?"

"He believed. But let me explain it this way," said Amor-el. "When you were giving birth to your first son, did you have faith that you would live through the experience?"

"Yes." I said.

"But what did it *feel* like?" said Amor-el

"Oh. I *thought* I was going to die," I said, humbled. "I understand. It is a happy event that can only come through pain. It is worth it after the pain is over, but the experience is terrifying. It really felt as though my body was splitting and that I was going to die."

Amor-el nodded and spoke to me, "You will hear Him cry out, "'My God, my God, why have you forsaken me?'" (Matt. 27:46, ESV). Jesus knows that He will die, but it seems to Jesus that He will be *eternally* dead. Shut out from life forever. Every appearance was against Him. He did not feel the presence or approval of His Father. He searched His mind for any rebellious thoughts or actions against God. Nothing. But no token of approval came from the Father. The final struggle was whether Jesus had enough faith in the character of God that He could submit Himself to eternal annihilation if God thought it was best. Jesus can leave men to suffer eternal death which is the consequence of their sin or He can take responsibility for solving a cosmic problem, go through this terrible ordeal, and allow Himself to sink into what appears to be eternal annihilation, but He cannot save Himself from this agony and hope to earn the right of restoration for mankind. God's Word told Him of a promised resurrection (Isa. 53:11; John 2:19), but He *felt* that He was to die along with the rest of mankind because the taint of the sin of humanity was on Him though He never sinned. He had overcome every inherited tendency to sin, but He was still human— one with the doomed race. Should He follow His feelings *or* should He follow His faith in God's loving character, in the promises in God's Word and the past experiences with His Father? If God saw that it would be best for Him to die eternally, should He be willing? Was He so contaminated by His humanity that it *would* be best for Him to die eternally? All these thoughts assaulted His mind. Satan had access to His mind as he had in the wilderness, only now in addition, Satan used the people around Jesus to mentally torture and speak Satan's words to Him—people that Jesus intensely loved with a love born of God."

I sobbed, "It probably seemed from living with humans for those thirty-three years that His humanity *should* lock Him out of heaven. Man's cruelty is terrible. Look how He's being treated! For what? That is His reward for healing people's sickened bodies and their even sicker minds?"

"Separation from God causes cruelty and hatred," said Amor-el. "All through His life Jesus taught men to love one another. Love the Romans. Love the Samaritans. Love sinners. Love God. They murdered Him for that. Unless they felt they stood to benefit in some way from Jesus, humanity hated His teaching that God's law demanded that they love one another. Except for those submitted in *some* measure to the Holy Spirit, all hated Him. But despite it all, in the garden, Jesus submitted Himself to God. If He used His divine power to save Himself from falling into the death that awaited Him, Satan would have won the controversy. Jesus would have established, by His action, the principle that it is not safe to trust God and that selfishness should be the ruling principle of life because God is not trustworthy. But Jesus set His path on the bloody course and was willing to die eternally, if it was the Father's will. Jesus, who had perfect knowledge of God, trusted the Father in the most adverse circumstances that Satan, with God's permission, could devise."

The hooting, hollering, and accusations against Jesus continued. The crosses were smeared by the feces of the condemned ones and the fun continued.

"Look," said Amor-el tenderly. "This is the final struggle with sin. After the long night of betrayal by men,

Satan continues to harangue Jesus. He has been stripped naked, bleeding, humiliated, exhausted, and in intense mental agony. Every breath is painful. He sees His mother. She knows who He really is and where He came from, but there is disappointment and anguish in her eyes. Though He has told her and the disciples repeatedly, she does not seem to be able to comprehend His mission. Seemingly abandoned by God, her eyes betray her feelings that He has failed. She believes that God, truly Jesus' Father, has abandoned Him. She believes Jesus' mission—His exalted mission—is over, failed. The other women shriek and cry. The disciples watch from a distance, afraid to come close. They also feel that His mission is a terrible failure, and they fear for their own lives. The only human encouragement comes from the words of faith from a dying thief—one of the men crucified next to Him. Only the thief appreciates Jesus' gentle character. The thief acknowledges that he is a sinner, unworthy, but asks to be a part of this new kingdom, this spiritual kingdom led by a loving King. He would feel safe if Jesus were the regent. "'[R]emember me when you come into your kingdom'" (Luke 23:42, ESV). These were words of affirmation and hope for Jesus. The thief clung to the faint hope that this honest man might be telling the truth and he voiced his hope that Jesus' gentle kingdom is the one in which he wanted to live. Satan planted his minions around Jesus, but God planted this honest but erring soul next to His Son as an encouragement." Amor-el added, "What a privilege that man had to encourage our dying Prince Jesus."

I was stunned that anyone thought being crucified was a privilege, even if it might be being crucified next to Jesus. I would have to begin seeing things from a different, more cosmic perspective. *I need to be more like Amor-el,* I thought. I returned my thoughts to the gruesome scenes before us.

Amor-el continued, "Satan is unrelenting. His own existence is at stake. He urged himself upon Jesus furiously and with cunning, 'Is it worth giving Your life for one person—for a thief? If You are successful, You will be the Savior of one. Even those with You for three-and-a-half years have rejected You. Your own mother believes You failed. Where is her faith? She who knows Your miraculous birth. Is this worth *Your* eternal life? Of what value is a dead savior, when You can live and influence the world for good and make it like heaven on earth? So, come down from the cross and all will *have* to believe You. Continue to do good to others instead of throwing Your life away. Is this pointless death what God truly wants? You are mistaken. Don't throw Your eternal life away. Would Your Father actually be pleased with this kind of foolishness?' But Jesus rejected all of Satan's thoughts and relied by faith on His Father's perfect will."

I watched as men taunted Jesus with Satan's words, "He saved others, himself he cannot save" (Matt. 27:42, Darby).

The crowd snickered and jeered. "Destroy this temple and in three days raise it up" (Matt. 26:61, paraphrase). "Hah! He is an imposter and a liar." They spit at Him and laugh hilariously. "Come down from the cross and we will believe You." They continued, inspired by Satan, "That man boasted about resurrection. He will never see such a day! His despicable body will be forever buried. God has abandoned Him. God may have protected Him before but look at Him now! How accurately does our law say, 'Cursed is everyone that hangs on a tree' [Gal. 3:13, paraphrase]. This is a fitting end for such a liar, for One cursed by our God!"

Overcome with emotion, Amor-el nearly whispered, "Satan continued to torment Jesus as much as he could, whispering to His mind the doubts he had presented to

Him through His life, but now with all the cunning force he could exert. 'Show them who You are. Just show them once. Just once. This stubbornness of Yours is thoughtless—leading to ruin, the ruin of the whole world. These people need a demonstration of power. But then, remember that You brought all this upon Yourself anyway. You brought all this suffering not only on Yourself but on the whole world. You *are* a criminal. But then, perhaps God's law of love is not sacred, surely even self-sacrificing love may have some exceptions. Who said that You need to obey God in *every* particular? Maybe it would be more loving to stay alive and heal the people. Think of how much more good You could do alive than dead. Surely a loving God does not actually mean that You should give Yourself over to death! Isn't this self-murder? Isn't it a sin? Is God testing You to see if You will commit self-murder? Is God testing You to see if Your love will put the world before loyalty to Him. Perhaps that is what He really wants. Sometimes You just cannot trust the plain Word of God. He may merely be testing You as He did Abraham. It wouldn't take much to come down from the cross. Allow Yourself to fall into death as any common man and *You* will die eternally. *You* have no Savior. You have been tainted by contact with sin all of Your life. You have a will that is separate from God's will. Think of it. You may be so tainted that He may never call You from the dead despite His *conditional* promises. Are You sure You can trust what is in the Torah and the prophets? Can You trust Your past experiences? No one cares about what You are doing. But really, You are worth *all* of them. You can create a new world to replace them. Just put them to sleep. It won't even hurt them. They won't even know." The voice whispers on, relentlessly. "Can You trust God? Can You trust God? Is this really from Your loving Father? Is such humiliation really from God?"

Jesus' response to Satan's temptations was, "Mother, Mary, John, Peter, James, Matthew, the soldiers, the sinner crucified next to Me … so many, so many. But if even one responds I cannot give that one up. Father, I know that You will not give them up. I know that is what You are like. I cannot give them up if there is the faintest hope that they will be restored to Us. According to Your Word there is hope for them. I trust You. I trust You. Father, do not let Me go. I trust in You."

"Look at Satan's final despicable temptation," said Amor-el. "Jesus thirsts. Instead of water He is offered a numbing potion. Satan knew that Jesus needed as clear a mind as possible to resist Satan's temptations, so one of his agents offered an escape from the tormenting thoughts and pain. But Jesus is victorious over even that temptation."

With a shudder, the voice of Jesus is heard, "It is finished. Father into Thy hands I entrust my Spirit!" (Luke 23:46, paraphrase).

Amor-el said, "Jesus rested in God and carried out His understanding of duty and obedience to the end. A hush of reverence blanketed the whole watching universe. Then we finally understood that Satan had been a liar and the seeds of murder were in him from the very beginning. His conduct at the cross was what God had predicted. Jesus did not *want* to sin—ever. Unlike your first parents who were protected from Satan everywhere but at the tree of the knowledge of good and evil, Jesus was hounded and provoked continually while on earth. Through Jesus, we saw that God was love, enduring the most horrible of temptations ever conceived, for you, Anne. God's nature truly is self-sacrificing love and not selfishness as Satan lied. Satan was that selfishness that would kill even his own Maker. We finally understood it all at the cross."

Amor-el's face nearly glowed as he said, "Then the cry of victory unheard by human ears rang throughout the entire universe. 'God is love. The universe rests secure. The Creator would give His very life for *one* of His creatures. Our lives are just as precious to God as is His own to Himself.' We all revered and loved Him more than ever."

Amor-el was beaming and I gladly joined him.

Amor-el continued, "All of the worlds resounded with the joy that God is truly unbounded, lavish love. The loyal beings then understood without any room for doubt that true freedom and love is total self-surrender to God. Now we had a deeper appreciation for the sacredness of love. The cross was a revelation of the pain that God has felt from sin's inception, but that is something even *we* could not appreciate until we saw the experience that Jesus went through; though the loyal ones had never sinned after the manner of the earth, we had never loved in the manner of the Creator. The extent of one's pain at rejection is the measure of one's love. Observing the life of Jesus on earth, we understand why you earthlings purposely shield yourself from pain by withholding love. God does none of that; it is against His very nature. He loves us too much to shield Himself from pain."

I felt barriers to love falling from my shoulders. I wanted to be like Jesus—to love God and to love my enemies. But what did it mean? I stopped. I thought of Satan.

"I think I asked this before, but even after the terrible cross, does God love Satan? And all of Satan's followers?" I asked.

"Of course. How lovingly did Jesus treat Judas? God continues to suffer over Lucifer and his followers. He has given them every chance to repent and return. But

He hates what they have become and the pain they have caused."

"I sensed that would be your answer to my question," I said. "But I understand why God has to put an end to this awful rebellion. Obviously, Satan didn't relent even after the cross. Did *you* think Satan would give in after the cross and tell God that He was right and that he was sorry and wrong for what he had done? It seems to me that he totally lost every argument at the cross."

"Some of us expected Satan and the rebellious angels to return to God and become obedient," said Amor-el. "But they continued to fight against God. We still did not understand the total power of pride and hatred which had overtaken them. Pride is the root of every sin."

"Pride is the root of all sin?" I questioned.

"Yes, pride. Pride is just another name for the principle that puts the individual first before God and before others. You might call it a disease except that when it is apparent that one's pride is hurting others, it is a choice—that is to say, sin," moaned Amor-el.

The End of the Conflict

"**A**mor-el," I said.

"Yes," Amore-el answered.

"Weren't all of Satan's accusations answered at the cross? Why are we still on earth? I mean, isn't this awful conflict over?" I asked.

"Almost. There is one very important unanswered question," said Amor-el.

"So, Satan continues to fight against God while this question is being answered?" I asked. "It must be pretty important."

"Exceedingly, overwhelmingly important or God wouldn't allow this suffering to continue. Take a look over there," pointed Amor-el.

I saw Satan amidst the shouts of triumph in heaven. "Wait, now. Jesus was unique. God's Son," he exploded, extreme anger on his handsome face. "The rest of this undeveloped race on earth cannot overcome sin in the way that God wants them to. They are steeped in rebellion. They have tasted of the freedom of rebellion against God. They can never, never change. God will have to change His law to accommodate them if He ever wants to have a relationship with them! They will never accept the Holy Spirit dwelling in them. Their very beings will recoil against such a thing. This law of self-sacrificing love will need to be changed to accommodate them." He paused and pulled back his shoulders. "But law, law—my law of goodness through inner growth—is acceptable and right. When I come to earth to reveal myself as a righteous lawgiver, then we will compare and see who succeeds and gains the love of the inhabitants. I will set up a kingdom of righteousness such as has never been seen before. I will set up a kingdom of greatness. The earth has had opportunity to see that lawbreaking only leads to disaster. The earth will bow, and I will teach all mankind righteousness. We will all work together in harmony. The way of self-determination, autonomy, and law can work! Men can overcome their cruelty and be moral individuals. We need education and law. We do *not* need God's Spirit to rule over us—only law. Morality is just as good as being controlled by the Holy Spirit. Men can *choose* by their own reasoning power to be good. No one needs to be encumbered by God's Spirit and give up his freedom. Not angels and not men. And these people who purport to follow Jesus because they love Him, will never *really* do so. They are steeped in self-centeredness. God's law is unfair. They were designed by God for destruction because they *cannot* accept His Spirit and live by His law. They live only by my law."

Satan continued, "When I prove my point and win the controversy and God changes the environment on earth—abolishing death—we can rule ourselves in righteousness. I will take control of the earth now and show the universe how many *supposed* followers of God will be loyal to Him—how many will follow His Spirit and the law of self-sacrificing love! None! God is *not* able to bring these so-called people of His to fruition. If God does save these people, He will have to relax His law of self-sacrificing love. He *cannot* bring them to fruition. They will not accept His tyrannical Spirit living in them," said Satan.

I was shocked at his tirade. I anticipated that Satan would show some humility and a sense of defeat. "Good grief. He is unrelenting. Is this the issue in the final battle on earth? Is it in the book of Revelation?" I asked.

"Yes," said Amor-el. "Satan means to have an earth loyal to him and to prove that people, even people saying that they love God, *cannot* be loyal to God. He wants to prove that morality is as acceptable to humanity as the righteousness that comes from God and that love for God is not enough to bring God's people to total acceptance of His Spirit and total self-surrender. Satan says that this applies to any created being—human or angel—none of us can keep the law of God, that we cannot reflect God's character."

> *If people are good because they accept moral principles, why is that not good enough?*

"Well, what *is* the difference? I'm confused. If people are good because they accept moral principles, why is that not good enough? Why isn't God satisfied with that?" I asked.

"Yes, I understand your dilemma," said Amor-el. "Anne, consider God's original design of connection with Him through the Holy Spirit and how much mere morality deviates from it. I will explain further. A man without God's Spirit can only do good deeds for selfish reasons, but selfishness is still the central principle in life. Having to choose between himself and others, he will always choose what benefits himself. God's character is self-sacrificing love. After the sacrifice on the cross, we knew that God would give Himself for each one of us. We finally understood that *only* that principle can bring eternal peace and harmony. And that we ourselves must live by that principle daily. But only God's Spirit can lead us in that path because only He lives within the realm of total love. Though the loyal angels were obedient to God's Spirit and never questioned His leading, we did not understand entirely the all-encompassing nature of the principle of true love. Only the cross was able to show us that. In one stroke at the cross, God revealed the nature of His character and the nature of sin."

I looked again at the beauty around me, but I was in agony. "But what blindness has come over the earth!" I shook my head. "So few understand the real character of God. Jesus' death was nearly 2,000 years ago. It's hard enough to believe it even happened, not to mention what it means. It's apparent that people haven't gotten the message."

"Satan continues to attempt to blind the eyes of earthlings," my guide explained. "After God's true nature of love was revealed at the cross, Satan worked to obscure that revelation of His character. To this day, many people serve God out of fear instead of love."

"I know. When I was a kid, I tried to obey God because I was afraid of burning in hell forever. It didn't work very well because it didn't make me *want* to obey God. But it sure made me miserable. I couldn't see God's love reflected in an eternally burning hell—burning someone forever for a relatively short lifetime of sin."[16]

Amor-el winced, "As though the character and love of God would not be enough to keep men from sinning, men have devised tales about an eternally burning hell. It is truly an insult to God. Many, many lies have been spread about Him. But human tales and traditions are hard to dispel. In spite of all of these deceptions, do not fear. There have always been people who sought God with all their hearts. God does not leave them without an answer, or without help. And there will come a time soon when God will have a people that love Him and desire to become one with Him and keep His principle of self-sacrificing love."

"Hmm. So even though the controversy over God's character was finished at the cross," I said, "God is allowing sin to continue to settle some remaining question or questions concerning created beings." I thought I understood, but I wanted to make sure, so I asked, "How will that happen?"

"There is one remaining question before the universe," said the angel. "God's purpose is to restore and reunite with humans. The question is this: 'Can created beings so totally trust God that they make choices contrary to their selfish nature?'"

> *"You are mistaken. This isn't just any book."*

"Haven't people already done that during the times of religious persecution?" I asked.

"Ah, but these times will be different," said Amor-el. "At the time of the end there will be an overwhelming delusion that God allows.[17] Only those who have fortified their minds with the Word of God will not be deceived. It will seem to the world that Jesus has arrived with messages from the Father—messages that are contrary to God's Word, contrary to the Bible."

"So what?" I asked. "If Jesus were to come back to earth and says something contrary to the Bible, then that's that. He is more of an authority than any book."

"You are mistaken. This isn't just any book," said Amor-el. "It is a revelation of God's character and His dealing with men and rebellion, set in writing, so that no one can say that it has been changed. The Word stands as a witness. When He was on earth, Jesus testified to His full acceptance of the Old Testament, with no equivocation. And His life was a fulfillment of the Old Testament. The New Testament is a witness to His life being the fulfillment of the Old Testament. The Bible should be carefully studied and cherished. Jesus warned you to study so that you would not be deceived."

"Deceived?" I said with a shudder. I now had a better understanding of the character of the deceiver, and it frightened me.

Amor-el continued, "Have you never read that there is a great test coming for God's people? That there is a mark of Satan's authority in opposition to God's authority? It is written in the Bible that a great test is coming on those living just before Jesus returns to the earth to gather His people (Rev. 13:7, 17). In the Book it is written 'and they loved not their lives unto the death.'[18] You humans deal loosely with words but God does not. Death means just that—death—not life. It was that way with Jesus, and it will be that way with God's restored people. As Satan devised the mental torture of the cross for Jesus and the circumstances surrounding His crucifixion, he hopes to devise nothing less for God's people to pry them away from loving and trusting in God. Do not be deceived."

"But that sounds like what Jesus did. Doesn't that elevate the creature to an almost God-like status just as Satan wanted in the beginning?" I asked.

Amor-el responded vigorously, "Oh, no, never. But it does show the power of God when indwelling a selfish being and His power to create a restored and an eternally secure universe."

"But I don't think people can be perfect!" I said, wagging my head in protest.

"Don't worry," said Amor-el. "Your test is not perfection. God will see to your growth. Your test is whether you love God enough to desire to change and to submit yourself to Him. God will do the changes in you. People have nothing of which to boast. The test is this: Can a sinful human understand that God is the measure of righteousness and not mankind and then surrender himself/herself to God's authority? With the light of God's character fully illuminated by Jesus, God's people will have a final test. Satan will exert the utmost pressure on those loyal to God. But God has told us in the Holy Scriptures, '[H]ere are they that keep the commandments of God, and [have] the faith of Jesus.'[19] They have the name of the Father 'written in their foreheads.'[20] They are totally committed to God's authority."

"Really?" I asked. "What kind of a test can that be?"

"God's people must keep the commandments of God through the power of the Holy Spirit. Motivated by their love for God, they will reach out in faith for power to be conformed to His likeness. They will keep *all* the commandments of God," said Amor-el. "Embedded in God's commandments is a test of loyalty. It speaks of God's power to create and God's power to redeem and restore. It is something that Satan does not want anyone to be reminded of. Satan will make it impossible, without God's Spirit, to keep that law," said Amor-el. "Just as the laws of the land and the rulers were arrayed against Jesus, so Satan will see to it that the laws of the earth are arrayed against God's people."[21]

I scoured my mind to think what commandment Amor-el was talking about. *Loyalty, creation, redemption?* Suddenly light came to my mind. "The Sabbath commandment," I blurted out. Immediately, I thought about how inconvenient it would be to keep the Sabbath day. I felt flush. I have three boys to support. I sometimes *had* to work on Sunday! A fitting test, indeed. Hadn't the Jews been hated and persecuted for keeping the Sabbath? I bet my kids will hate me for keeping it too. But I decided that God knew best. I would be obedient.

I thought for a moment and then said, "But are only those saved who pass 'the test—those who are alive on earth when the test comes—those who keep Sunday holy?"

"Not Sunday—the Sabbath—the seventh-day," winced Amor-el.

"Ohhhh," I spluttered out. "I thought that Christians now keep Sunday holy. I'm not sure why, except maybe that Jesus was resurrected on Sunday." I thought about how much more inconvenient and nearly impossible it would be to keep the seventh-day Sabbath. Then I remembered the character of the arch deceiver and admired the way he had prepared for the final test to be difficult.

"The Lord's commandments are unchangeable," said Amor-el solemnly. "The seventh day of the week is the Sabbath. It is a memorial of creation and redemption as stated in the commandments. It has never been changed by God, only by men." He paused. "This is the test of loyalty."

"But many Christians down through the centuries have not kept the Sabbath. Are they lost? That would be most unfair of God," I stated emphatically.

"No, they are not lost," said Amor-el. "But the faithful stand as representatives of all those who are saved. All who share their love for Jesus *would* have acted in the same way under the same circumstances."

"Oh, the same reason that Jesus' death can save every person! That kind of 'corporate principle,'" I said.

"Yes," said Amor-el. "This is the final battle ground—Armageddon. After this tremendous spiritual battle is over, your little world, once the center of rebellion against God, will become the dwelling place of God and the center of the universe." His face lit up with love and admiration for God. "There will be peace on earth and in the universe."

"Well, what happens to the little sinner?" I asked, smiling sheepishly. "You know. Not too bad. Not too good."

"God's law is complete truth and justice. One deliberate transgression is a violation of God's law. No one can transgress God's law and be in His presence unless, through repentance, he asks for forgiveness and wants to totally change. The Prince's sacrifice is complete. Forgiveness and acceptance are assured."

I looked again at the beautiful surroundings with longing. I thought, *Even my boys might love it here*. I corrected myself. *They actually might hate it here*. They needed some enlightenment and some love for God and His ways.

"OK, but what about those who don't know enough to ask for forgiveness, who have never even heard of Jesus?" I asked impatiently.

"The Holy Spirit stands as a witness to all. God knows who are His and who desire to know truth and walk in the way of obedience. That is not a problem for God," said Amor-el.

But there was one last nagging doubt about God that I needed to clear up. I asked, "So does God kill all the rebellious at the end of time? Isn't that what the Bible says? God kills them in a lake of fire?" I asked. "But that doesn't sound like something that Jesus would do."

"Sin and sinners will indeed come to an end," said Amor-el. "For nearly six thousand years, God has allowed sin to reign on your earth. Angels have watched, and it has become clear to them that there are some who would be miserable in heaven and who would rather die than live in His presence. Each decides during the course of their lives which master they will serve. This accomplished, God does His strange work. The rebellious receive what they themselves have chosen. By a life of rebellion, Satan and all who unite with him place themselves so out of harmony with God that His very presence is to them a consuming fire. The glory of Him who is love destroys them, by their own choice," said Amor-el.

I shuddered at the thought, because in the light of my past life, I felt so vulnerable. And what about my children? But now that the genesis of evil was crystal clear to me and God's justice and mercy in dealing with the rebellion was clear to me, solemnly, I said, "The cosmic trial will be over, the cosmic jury concludes that God *is* righteous, that creatures are defective without His Holy Spirit, God reveals Himself and each person has decided his own destiny whether they want to be with Him or would rather die. It is just and fair."

"Yes," Amor-el agreed. "Even Satan will acknowledge God's righteous way of putting down his rebellion. Every knee will bend before Him. Satan and his followers will choose to die rather than to live by God's righteous law. They continue to reject the person of God, the Holy Spirit, who is life," said Amor-el. "It is very, very sad. But thankfully the reign of sin and terror will soon end. Many have fought off the Holy Spirit so many times that they cannot live in His presence. The judgment at the lake of fire is not a legal one, but a revelation of the heart. God will never change anyone against his/her will. Men may have intellectually understood the Bible, but the life proves whether they have truly accepted salvation. The unrighteous have done their choosing during the course of their lives. Anne, it is dangerous to ignore the pleadings of God's Spirit even for a moment."

At this point, the love, mercy, and justice of God overwhelmed me. God's humility made me ashamed of my pride and selfishness. His mercy and fairness inspired me with a newborn love. His unwillingness to have His creatures live in anything but a gentle universe of total love, astounded me. I started to cry, uncontrollably. I felt profound sorrow for my previous rebellion. It was now clear why God allows sin and suffering and how He

Himself has borne the burden of sin and suffering. I had found the righteous, gentle God I thought did not exist.

Amor-el embraced me. "Your tears will turn to joy unspeakable as you continue to worship Jesus," he said. After what seemed to be an hour, I stopped crying. "Now go back and tell all these things to others on earth. Some will listen and understand," Amor-el said. "Do you want to have a part in helping people understand God's character?"

"Oh, yes," I nearly screamed.

"So, you must go back to earth. Soon, soon the night of sorrow and sin will be over, and God will make all things new."

"What does God specifically want me to do?" I asked.

Amor-el gently stated, "God Himself will show you what to do. Stay close to Him. Pray without ceasing. You must return to your children now. May the goal of your life be to live with Jesus forever and to spread His love to all those around you."

When he finished speaking, a bright light surrounded us and I shut my eyes. When I opened them again, I was at home and it looked very, very dark to me. But love for my boys filled my mind and heart. I nearly ran through the house to find them. It was breakfast time and amazingly they were all assembled at the kitchen table, looking very hungry. I nearly exploded, "I have something glorious, wonderful to tell you! Please listen to me."

"Oh, Mom," they groaned.

Notes

[1] Batchelor, Doug, and David Boatwright. "WHO IS MICHAEL THE ARCHANGEL?" Amazing Facts. https://1ref.us/1v2 (accessed February 22, 2022).

[2] Rittenour, Curtis. "'LUCIFER' — DARK LIES." Amazing Facts. https://1ref.us/1v3 (accessed February 22, 2022).

[3] Batchelor, Doug, and Kim Kjaer. "THE TRINITY: IS IT BIBLICAL?" Amazing Facts. https://1ref.us/1v4 (accessed February 22, 2022).

[4] "The Divinity of the Holy Spirit." Amazing Facts. https://1ref.us/1v5 (accessed February 22, 2022).

[5] Rittenour, Curtis. "IS THERE LIFE ON OTHER WORLDS?" Amazing Facts. https://1ref.us/1v6 (accessed February 22, 2022).

[6] Genesis 3:15.

[7] Joshua 2:1; Matthew 1:5.

[8] 2 Samuel 12:1–10.

[9] Matthew 4:1–11.

[10] Strobel, Lee. "The Case for a Creator." *YouTube*, uploaded by mina Paul, September 12, 2013, https://1ref.us/1v7 (accessed February 22, 2022) and Strobel, Lee. "The Case for Christ." *YouTube*, uploaded by mina Paul, September 12, 2013, https://1ref.us/1v8 (accessed February 22, 2022).

The case for Creation. The Case for Christ. Apologetic Series by Lee Strobel.

[11] Compare Exodus 10:1 and Exodus 10:20 with Exodus 7:14, Exodus 8:15, and Exodus 9:35.

[12] The author acknowledges total scientific ignorance on her part and the silence of the Bible regarding the reason for the flood except that men were exceedingly wicked and God permitted the flood. An omniscient God has no need to be fickle and "change His mind" about creation and decide to do away with most people on earth by flooding it. There always seems to be a relationship between the disasters that God allows and man's sin or, in the alternative, some kind of demonstration in the controversy between God and Satan. (See Job chapter 1 and Job 2:1–8.) The Bible does compare the last days and the time of Noah (Matthew 24:37). Assuming that we are in the last days and considering that we are capable of self-annihilation, it seems plausible to the author that the flood was caused by men. Also God has a history of protecting His people during destruction. Consider Noah and Lot (Genesis 6–8, 14, and 19).

[13] Consider the record in Genesis 5 that men lived much longer pre-flood than after the flood.

[14] Exodus 23:28; Joshua 24:12.

[15] The sacrifice of Jesus is seen in symbolism in the Jewish feasts and ceremonial law. "God Drew the Plans." Amazing Facts. https://1ref.us/1v9 (accessed February 22, 2022).

[16] "Hell Truth Q&A." Hell Truth. https://1ref.us/1va (accessed February 22, 2022).

[17] 2 Thessalonians 2:9–12; Matthew 24:24.

[18] Revelation 12:11.

[19] Revelation 14:12.

[20] Revelation 14:1.

[21] White, Ellen G. *The Great Controversy Between Christ and Satan* (Mountain View, CA: Pacific Press Publishing Association, 1911). This volume traces the controversy between Christ and Satan through the ages.

TEACH Services, Inc.

P U B L I S H I N G

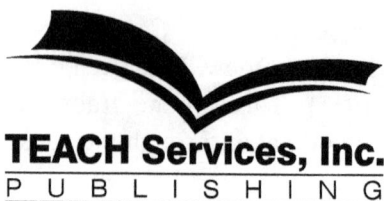

We invite you to view the complete
selection of titles we publish at:
www.TEACHServices.com

We encourage you to write us
with your thoughts about this,
or any other book we publish at:
info@TEACHServices.com

TEACH Services' titles may be purchased in
bulk quantities for educational, fund-raising,
business, or promotional use.
bulksales@TEACHServices.com

Finally, if you are interested in seeing
your own book in print, please contact us at:
publishing@TEACHServices.com

We are happy to review your manuscript at no charge.